ZEN DIARY

ZEN DIARY

by Paul Wienpahl

HARPER & ROW, PUBLISHERS
NEW YORK, EVANSTON, AND LONDON

LIBRARY OF CONGRESS CATALOG CARD NUMBER: 70-109059

For Janet

CONTENTS

THIS BOOK IS COMPANION TO *The Matter of Zen,* WHICH APPEARED in 1964. It presents inner aspects of that to which the other gave the outer form. Therefore there is no need here for acknowledgments; they were given there. However, a few preliminary remarks are necessary.

As the title suggests, the book is autobiographical. I have tried to keep descriptive material and footnotes to a minimum. Chapter One is an exception, which will be explained. In the accomplishment of this purpose an Appendix has been provided. It should be read before turning to Chapter II. Philosophical references are for the most part explained in Chapter I. Others which concern Zen Buddhism, such as those to Rinzai, a Chinese teacher of the ninth century, may be found in *The Matter of Zen.*

In this vein there are quotations from Wittgenstein and paraphrases of him which are often not identified. Those familiar with his work will recognize them. I have not documented them, since these phrases rang in my mind and I doubt whether I could locate them even if this were important.

Chapter I is also autobiographical, although it does not look it because of its apparent scholarship. It represents in two parts those aspects of my intellectual life which led to the writing of *Zen Diary.* The first half expresses my frame of mind in the 1950's; the second, things that shook that structure. Since the chapter is a man's story and not a history, I have not dealt with movements in contemporary philosophy which do not bear on what follows. Nor do I more than mention some of the men who particularly influenced me, since they do not appear in the *Diary*. I think particularly here of G. E. Moore and John Wisdom—of what they did and the manner in which they did it. (The *style* as well as the substance of some twentieth-century philosophers is important.)

Because it is autobiographical, Chapter I will sound odd, stilted, and repetitive. This could not be helped. As I say, it represents my frame of mind at one stage. However, horrible as this picture of it is, I believe that the state of mind is common, or was, in those of my generation. This curious picture is the result of my particular background.

Whether the account of issues and men in Chapter I jibes with other interpretations of them does not matter. It is the story of my intellectual life. And, I must add, it was a relief to be able to write it without having for once to check for accuracy and objectivity—to be able to feel: this is the way I read them. For these reasons logical arguments gradually play a lesser role in this chapter. I was changing.

For the reader who would like to know more about this change, there is an essay I wrote in 1955 called "Philosophical Reflections." It was published in the summer of 1959 in the *Chicago Review*. During those years I found myself without a philosophical position. I still have none. But that was an intellectual accomplishment. It needed grounding in a practice. It had to become more of me than an idea. We are kind by *being* kind.

Then the Zen study commenced, first with books and finally in practice. And I began to appreciate the fact that philosophical problems are not solved. They can only be dissolved. A man knows all, understands, when he no longer has any questions—not when he has all the answers. The limits of philosophy are mysticism. I'm not there, but I can see the destination.

Finally, I wish to say that Freud does not often appear in this book. I knew about him. But I have only latterly come to appreciate him. Anyway, how could you possibly get what he does into a book—really any more than you can get philosophy and a life into a book?

Santa Barbara   P.W.
1969

Which of you by taking
thought can add one
cubit unto his stature?
　　—Matthew 6:27

WESTERN PHILOSOPHY DURING THE PAST HUNDRED YEARS SEEMS to me to have consisted in attempts to see through idealism. Important essays in this process, such as G. E. Moore's "The Refutation of Idealism," suggest by their content, if not always by their titles, that the concern of the contemporary philosopher has been the *refutation* of idealism. Kierkegaard's critical claim that the secret of modern philosophy lies in the identification of thought with being, Dewey's notion that *the* philosophic fallacy is the identification of the objects of knowledge with ultimately real things, and Sartre's summarizing statement that existence precedes essence similarly suggest that the task has been the refutation of idealism. Nevertheless, it seems to me that it has been that of seeing through idealism rather than that of refuting it.

I think, too, that the task has been wider and deeper than has appeared. For the term "idealism" very likely refers to a whole frame of mind as well as to the view which has been precisely defined as metaphysical idealism. I am not sure of all aspects of this frame of mind, but I believe that it includes the following beliefs, tendencies, and deep-seated assumption. They do not appear to be logically related, but are connected rather as parts of a building are.

The beliefs are: (1) that the real (world) is rational (the world is spirit), (2) Cartesian dualism (the mind and the body are distinct substances), (3) Platonism (there is a realm of becoming and a realm of being, or essences), (4) that philosophy will make all the difference in life, and (5) that if we look

I

long enough and carefully enough we will get the truth about the world (all our questions will be answered).

The tendencies in idealism are: (1) to obliterate the distinction between the subjective and the objective (the I and the thou), and (2) to intellectualism. There is finally a deep-seated assumption about the relation of language to fact, about the way language works. I call this the assumption of the naming relation. It is embodied in a more general assumption about man's relation to the world.

Some of the Elements of the Logic of Metaphysical Idealism

In the seventeenth century, men who thought reflectively felt gnawing skepticism and doubt.[1] The medieval outlook no longer sufficed. In Descartes' metaphor, the tree of knowledge was without roots. The philosophic task appeared to be the discovery of these roots. A metaphysic was needed, and Descartes provided it.[2]

He reasoned as follows. When he reflected on his condition he found that fundamentally he could doubt all that he believed How, for example, did he know that his senses did not deceive him or that he was not dreaming all the time? How, then, did he know that there was a world out there? And, if there were not, what of all the so-called truths of science? Furthermore, suppose he had been created by some evil demon and not God, as he had always thought? Such a demon could have made him so that he was not only deceived about the world, but even that there *was* a world. He could have so created Descartes that he believed that 2 x 2 = 4 whereas it might equal 5.

In the welter of confusion which this reasoning produced, however, Descartes found one thing he could not doubt. He could not doubt that he doubted. This flash of light came to be called the *Cogito* argument; for, since doubting is a form of thinking, the light came to be expressed as "I think, therefore I am" (*Cogito ergo sum*).

Descartes then proceeded by easy, though not so convincing, stages to uncover the other roots of the tree of knowledge, the other sure principles on which the rest of his knowledge could be based. He saw that he was sure of himself as a being that thinks. Whether he had a body was still open to doubt. However, as he examined his ideas, the essence of a thinking being was to "entertain" ideas, he found one which differed from all the rest in peculiar and noteworthy respects. This was the idea of God. For one thing, it was so forceful that it seemed impossible that its object, God, did not exist. How *could* there be no Creator? For another, how could anything but a Perfect Being have caused the idea of one? A cause must be equal to its effect. Thus did Decartes come to his second principle, that God, the Perfect Being, exists.

Notice how Descartes is moving from the field of doubt back to the realm in which he had formerly believed. Despite its appearance of logic, you may question the validity of his reasoning. But it is clear that it allayed his doubts. It is common practice in the schools today to demonstrate that no freshman would succeed in a class in philosophy if he handed in Descartes' *Meditations* as a term paper. Nevertheless, his line of reasoning satisfied one of the great mathematicians of all time. This is explicable when you consider the possibility that there is more to a philosophical argument than logic. It helps here to think of "proofs" in a court of law. However we regard this, it is a fact that Descartes was able to settle his last great doubt, that there was a physical world (as well as his mental one), by probing the ground for yet another root with the new tools he had.

If he was created by God, and of that he was now sure, then it was impossible that he had been deceived in his earlier belief that there is a physical world in which things move, in which there are other people, and in which he and they exist as a physical as well as mental creatures. And now he sees that he has the basic truths he needs to believe all the rest. He exists, God exists, and the physical world exists.

Whether others were convinced by Descartes' agruments is open to question. Certainly many capable contemporaries, even as the freshman today, tore his arguments to shreds. Nevertheless, Descartes' views about what exists and what it is basically like became the common property of European men, and today we speak of him as the father of modern philosophy.

There are many reasons for this in addition to the doubtful logic of his conclusions. For one thing, Descartes expressed in clear terms a basic and simple outlook which had long been developing in the West. There is the world which God created, and there are the people in it, who are distinct from all other creatures in that they gradually come to know about this world. The rational animals. For another thing, Descartes' sharp distinction between the two kinds of "things" in the natural world, the mental and the physical, unhooked Western man from a profound dilemma he had come consciously to face with the development of modern science. How could he at the same time be a freely acting creature (which is necessary for all his hopes and aspirations, especially the moral ones) and live in a world that is causally ordered (which is necessary if science, knowledge, is to be possible—and who could doubt then that it was)? Descartes provided the answer: the physical world is the province of science. In it there are the causal relationships described in the laws of science. The mental "world" is the province of freedom.[3]

However, this common-sense view of the world has a fatal flaw with which we have struggled ever since.[4] It separates the subjective from the objective (enables us to be objective, scientific), and though it removes values from the "world," it somehow preserves them. But in doing so it separates man from his world. It not only makes man an alien in his world, but alienates him from his fellows and ultimately from himself. The realization of this has been slow in dawning, though Descartes himself had a deeply disturbing glimmer of it. It occurred to him in the form of what philosophers call the problem of interaction, or the mind-body problem. In its poorly felt but somehow precisely understood form it was stated by Descartes: How can the mind and the body interact, since they are completely different substances?

The flaw soon came to have another form, as reflective men turned from the problem apparently solved by Descartes to a concern with the nature of science. They did this in the persons of Locke, Berkeley, and Hume. Impressed with the growing success of the physical scientist, Locke wondered whether the method of science could be applied to moral and political problems. This led him to an examination of the origin, nature, and limits of knowledge.

Among other things, Locke concluded that knowledge is a system of ideas which represent the laws governing the world, and that knowing consists in forming this system and checking its parts with what we observe. Ideas, he further concluded, come to us from sense experience. Since this is their origin, knowledge must therefore be limited to experience. This made Locke skeptical of any claims about the world which transcended experience (for example, about God the Creator).[5]

When you think about it you see that the model, so to speak, on which Locke's conclusions are based is the one to which Descartes gave full expression. According to it, the physical world is there, and our minds here. We come into this world and by observation become aware of the elements of its structure, which we then put together in thought to form knowledge. The model is dualistic. Continuing with the logic of this model, Hume carried it to its conclusion. He thereby exposed another facet of the deadening defect in Descartes' work. This is complete skepticism about the possibility of knowledge itself —which includes, of course, skepticism about (the knowledge of) values.

Hume's argument was simple, inexorable, and devastating. If knowledge comes from experience, then how can we be sure of any of our beliefs about the world? Suppose, for example, that I come across a footprint in the sand and infer (come to believe) that a human being has passed there. How can I know whether my belief is true, short of having seen him make the print? Well, if I knew that humans always make footprints like this, I could be sure of my inference. But how can I know that humans always make footprints like this one? (Notice that the proposition is typical of the laws of science.) I would have to know, not only that they have made them in the past, but that they will make them in the future. Clearly I would have to know something like the proposition that the future resembles the past; in other words, that there are causal laws. And the truth of that proposition obviously cannot be known if knowledge comes from experience. Since all inference, and consequently belief, rests on this principle which itself cannot be justifiably believed, it follows that knowledge is unobtainable. Hume, therefore, concluded that what we call knowledge is simply opinion based on custom and habit, both of which are clearly relative to time and circumstance.

Western philosophic thought came to a turning point with Hume. Kant made the turn with his self-styled "Copernican revolution." He saw that, although Hume's logic was unquestionable there was something dreadfully wrong with its outcome. For example, if Hume is right then science is impossible. Nevertheless, we do have science. Hume, in other words, confronts us with a paradox, which is a form of the flaw in Descartes' work.

As we get closer to our own day (to ourselves) we find that Kant has a less dry, a more emotional, way of expressing the flaw. If Hume is right, then morality is impossible, at least morality based on reason. On the other hand, probably the greatest human aspiration is that of knowingly doing good. If this aspiration is groundless, then human life is a mockery. (The trouble of our times, yours and mine, is deep-seated. Kant saw that there may be no hope in it. But he refused to accept this possibility.)

Kant resolved the paradox, and thereby opened the doors of contemporary philosophic thought. He did so by radically wrenching the model of human experience which Westerners have used since Socrates, and which we have seen consciously formulated by Descartes.[6]

Hume's conclusion that we cannot know that the future resembles the past was based on this model. Simply but profoundly, Kant changed it and produced a new model, according to which we do not experience a ready-made world. Instead, he supposed, we experience phenomena which are ordered in certain general ways by the action of our minds on whatever it may be "out there" that "stimulates" them. In other words what we experience, and hence come to know, is partly the result of our creation. What is "really" out there, beyond these phenomena, we cannot know.

Kant's very language now becomes hellishly complicated. There are "things-in-themselves" and "minds-in-themselves." Together he called them noumena. These somehow interact to produce the world of phenomena, the world in which we *as phenomena* have our existence as experiencing creatures. In this interaction the minds-in-themselves structure the phenomena. Thus it is that the world *as we experience it* is spatial, temporal,

7

qualitative, and above all causal in character. It has, in other words, a composition such that in it the future resembles the past. And it must have this composition or it would not be. Thus we know by Kant's hypothesis that the future resembles the past, at least in our experience, and the paradox presented by Hume's work dissolves.

There can be no doubt that Kant's new model does the job. It leaves us with the question, however, whether there is any reason to accept it. It took Kant twelve years to work out a justification and we need not go into it. Suffice to say that one aspect of it concerned a consequence of accepting the model. If the model is correct then knowledge is limited to phenomena; for only these, so far as we can know (by the model), are causally ordered. From this it follows that we can know nothing about things-in-themselves. In other words, we cannot know anything about the whole of reality. All metaphysical claims must, therefore, be impossible.

In this Kant went along with Locke and Hume. He was skeptical about some matters. And he proceeded to show that all statements which purport to be about the whole of reality that is, to include the noumena as well as the phenomena, are indeed impossible. He did this by showing that they are antinomies. He thus anticipated the work of the logical positivists who "demonstrated" that metaphysical claims are meaningless.[7] The profound skepticism in our Western development is becoming more articulated. In the twentieth century it has enabled W. H. Auden to describe ours as the "age of anxiety."

Kant's insight into human experience has other aspects beside that of rendering skepticism clearer. It made us acutely aware of the dualistic model which had been unconsciously forming in our minds for centuries. It showed us that the assumption that we come into a ready-made world was questionable, and this suggests the possibility of getting beyond all such assumptions. It also suggested the possibility that we are "responsible" for at least part of what we experience (for example, its order). And, finally, it showed us that the picture we have had of knowledge itself is open to question. We have thought that knowledge "told" us what the world is about. With Kant there looms the possibility that in knowing we are simply controlling experience.[8] The working out of Kant's insight becomes Hegelian idealism, pragmatism, logical positivism, and existentialism.

Metaphysical or Hegelian Idealism   Although it started in metaphysics, there is in the logic of idealism a growing distrust of metaphysics. Kant was even more explicit about this than Hume. The urge to know everything, he thought, is doomed to result in contradictions. It is the attempt that gives us science, but we must learn to control it. The turn away from a major tradition of Western thinking had been made.

Kant's immediate successors, particularly Hegel, started off in a new direction. There was logic even in this movement. For these men saw, as he himself had, that there was a fundamental contradiction in Kant's own work. Baldly put, it is this: According to Kant's critical philosophy there is causality only in the realm of phenomena. That is why we can know phenomena, but not noumena. On the other hand, it is part of the critical philosophy that the noumena "produce" the phenomena; that is, strictly speaking, cause them. We cannot, therefore, logically believe that there are noumena. Even Kant held that we can know nothing *about* them, although he believed that we can know by his critical work *that* they exist. The first logical step in the new direction, therefore, was to say "away with things-in-themselves," which leaves us only the phenomena.

Looking back, we can see that there was more than logic to this step. Ever since Descartes there had been a growing

9

awareness of the bankruptcy of the Western spiritual tradition. To alter the metaphor, there was a rapid development toward the flowering of something new, although it too had roots deep in the past.[9]

The step amounted to abandoning metaphysics in practice as well as theory. Hume and Kant had warned against it. Men, however, continued to speculate; men, that is, except Hegel, Schopenhauer, and a few others. These turned to the new task which Hegel called "the phenomenology of spirit."

The first step in the new direction was a big one, yet we faltered in making it.[10] There are no noumena, said Hegel. Let us investigate, then, only the phenomena, the appearances. He was starting the phenomenology of the individual human spirit. But he, or we, took this to be the phenomenology of Spirit. For to account for the appearances (the old tendency to seek knowledge of the All still prevailed), Hegel said that they are the workings of mind, ultimately the Absolute Mind. Reality is the process of Mind coming to complete self-consciousness. It begins as an unconscious Spirit. Then, by positing Its opposite, which is non-mind or matter, It moves by an awareness of this toward an awareness of Itself. Hegel then developed what more than appeared to be an elaborate metaphysics (old-style).

There is no need here to pay attention to the details of this system. They appear in Hegel's *The Phenomenology of Mind,* in which there is even an elaborate chart of the Absolute. Taken as parts of a metaphysics, they are bewildering. For they make everything we ordinarily take to be real (trees, grass, the waves of the ocean) to be but appearances which are the workings of Mind in its struggle toward self-consciousness.[11] When read as the inward turning of a mind, a person, describing the life of the spirit, these details are marvelously interesting and full of insight. But they were not so read in Hegel's time. Instead, reflective men entered by these doors into the Life of the Spirit. They confused the subjective with the objective and departed from their lives into a ghostly realm which they took to be The Real. As I say, doing metaphysics old-style continued to prevail.[12]

Contemporary Movements, Pragmatism During the nineteenth century there were developments other than Hegelianism. It was *the* era of natural science. Auguste Comte popularized the death of old-style metaphysics in his positivistic philosophy. Mill wrote philosophy without touching on metaphysics except to criticize that of others. Hegelianism moved in the schools to England and the United States. Darwin published *The Origin of Species*. And at the end of the century there was a philosophical reaction against absolute idealism.[13]

In 1909, on the fiftieth anniversary of *The Origin of Species,* John Dewey published his article "The Influence of Darwin on Philosophy." When Darwin's book originally appeared, people had seen in it a threat to Christianity. Fifty years later Dewey made it clear that the influence of the theory of evolution was far more profound than had initially been thought. It went to the deepest sources of the Western philosophical outlook.

People in the West had for twenty-four centuries thought and lived in terms of the Greek distinctions between appearance and reality, becoming and being, content and form. And they had regarded reality, being, and form as unchanging. This had given them their picture of knowledge, science: it is the awareness of reality, of form, of the unchanging. They had believed that opinion deals with what can change. The philosophic influence of Darwin's work was in the direction of completely abandoning this picture, and consequently the dualisms that go with it. For Darwin had demonstrated that we have no reason to believe in the immutability of forms. As Dewey saw it, we had as a result of this demonstration to change what he called our whole "logic." By this he meant our theory of knowledge. It is now clear that this also meant that we must give up metaphysics.[14]

The theory of knowledge which had to be changed or abandoned is old. It appeared in classical Greece and has in our time been called the representative theory. It has been expressed in many ways, or has worked simply as a deeply hidden assumption. According to this theory, knowledge is like a picture or a map which re-presents in the mind the structure of reality. It is true when the picture corresponds with its object, the map with its terrain. For the Greeks the value of knowledge lay, like that of a picture, in its aesthetic qualities. The highest form of life for a man consisted in the contemplation of knowledge.

However, if there are no forms, a structure, reality, to be pictured, what then is this thing we call knowledge, this action we call knowing? The clue for an answer to this question Dewey found in the theory of evolution, although the answer was already being worked out by James and C. S. Peirce along other lines. Knowledge, it seemed to Dewey, must be an instrument used by man in the struggle for existence. Knowing must be a way of adapting to the environment. Its function, then, is like that of any biological adaptation. And man's success as a specie indicates that it is an extremely useful adaptation.

Here is a new theory of knowledge. Popularly it has been called pragmatism. Professional philosophers prefer the term "instrumentalism." According to this theory, knowledge is made up of ideas or concepts and theories which string bits of experience to each other. Their function is that of enabling us to make predictions, given *this* experience to anticipate *that*. If the units of knowledge are to be compared to anything, they should be compared to tools. And like that of any tool, their test lies in whether they work. Thus, this new theory of knowledge embodies a new theory of truth. An idea, or better a theory, is true, not when it corresponds to some structure in reality, but when it works.

However, like the tendency to metaphysics old-style, its relative, the representative theory of knowledge forces its way in on us in face of this new development. It makes us want to say that a theory works because it is true. To have it the other way around simply isn't "reasonable." Therefore, James and Dewey had to struggle to make themselves clear to others, and probably to themselves. They did this by indulging in something that looked very much like metaphysics old-style (we still do not have a successful name for it, though "linguistic philosophy" is not bad). And they took this direction because their work had "metaphysical" implications; that is, the abandonment of metaphysics had to go along with it. As this becomes clear, so does the relation of metaphysics to mind-body dualism.

Dewey's writings after "The Influence of Darwin on Philosophy" work out the details of the new theory of knowledge and expose its implications.[15] In *Experience and Nature* he deals with the abandonment of metaphysics, although he does not express himself that way. He announces that his intention is the presentation of a new philosophy, which he will call either empirical naturalism or naturalistic empiricism. He continues by saying that the association of the two words "experience" and "nature" will seem to many people like talk of a round square. When you reflect that these terms are his versions of Descartes' "mind" and "body," and that Descartes felt it impossible that mind and body should interact, you see what Dewey was getting at. He then says that he knows of "no route by which dialectical argument can answer such objections. One can only hope in the course of the whole discussion to disclose the meanings which are attached to 'experience' and 'nature,' and thus insensibly produce, if one is fortunate, a change in the significations previously attached to them." (p. 1)[16]

There is no reason here why we should attempt the impossible. In our time Dewey, James, and Wittgenstein have tried it. Their works are there to be read. What these men are saying is simply put. But as with psychoanalysis, in which it does no good for the analyst to *tell* the patient that he is suffering from unresolved Oedipal conflicts, so here it does no good to say that what is involved is the abandonment of mind-body dualism, hence of the representative theory of knowledge, and hence of metaphysics old-style—which may now be seen as the attempt to provide a theory for bringing mind and body together again. Something like a psychoanalysis is needed, a lengthy analysis in depth.[17] For it is not just our intellects that are involved in dualism. Our entire condition as human beings is so involved. It is a consequence of dualism to believe that only our intellects are. Thus I proceed by turning to see what James had to say on these matters.

William James came to his philosophical undertaking from psychology via religious issues. In the United States in the last decades of the nineteenth century a revised version of the Bible had appeared, and "higher criticism" was imported from Germany. Agnosticism and atheism became matters of public concern. James found himself worrying about the belief in God. As a psychologist, he recognized its importance in people's well-being. On the other hand, there were the doubts about the truth of the belief, and there were the atheists.

James found a way of dealing with this difficulty in the will to believe. Recognizing that we cling to many of our beliefs for other than logical reasons, and that as long as they make our lives satisfactory we accept them, he saw in this the importance of the will to believe. It is often this will to believe a hypothesis that makes it work for us. He concluded, in effect, that it is all right to believe that God exists if we want to. Indeed, any belief is all right, provided that holding it does not harm others.

Clearly such a view demands clarification and justification. That the idea of God works for some people cannot mean that God exists—that is, that the idea that He does is true. So James moved on to what he called his pragmatism. This he regarded as a method of resolving metaphysical disputes. Its principle is that, if an idea can be shown to have practical results in our behavior, then it is true. And surely this is the case with the idea of God. However, clearly it is also the case that merely believing in God is no indication that He does in fact exist.

Thus, James had to go further—to a theory of truth. Truth, he held, is a property of ideas, at least some ideas. An idea is true when it corresponds with reality. False when it does not. However, James went on to examine this correspondence. As he did, it seemed to him that an idea "corresponds" to reality when it puts us into working touch with it, that is, when it is useful. Ideas are true when they lead us to anticipate results which eventually occur. There is, indeed, a correspondence between true ideas and realities, but it is not between something in our consciousnesses now and something "out there" now. It is a correspondence between the idea and some future experience—a correspondence between anticipated results and actual results, between an experience *now* and an experience *then*. A true idea is one which brings this correspondence about.

This led James to examine cognition. He found that one can distinguish between ideas and other "mental" phenomena such as memories, feelings, perceptions, and imaginings. Only ideas, which make up knowledge, have the property of truth. All the other mental phenomena are simply experiences which ideas relate to each other. There is nothing that corresponds to these experiences. They simply are. Memory is sight at a distance. A memory is no more true than a perception is. Hallucination is another kind of experience. We have been tricked, in comparing it to perception, into thinking that there are true and false perceptions.

By this route James arrived at his "radical empiricism." It was during this time that he wrote the letter quoted in note 4. The journey resulted in a collection of papers called *Essays in Radical Empiricism*. The first of these is "Does Consciousness Exist?" To this question James answered No. He had then to say something about the facts to which we refer by the word "conscious" and its derivatives. He had, in other words, to invent a new way of talking. The result was radical empiricism.

Again, I shall not repeat what is already in print. James came to picture the world, reality, as what he called "pure experience." The use of this phrase corresponds to that of the word "substance" in Spinoza' *Ethics,* although it has the subjective ring of Ernst Mach's "things are sensations." A handy way of seeing what James was getting at is in fact provided by Spinoza. Individual things, the latter said, are just modes, modifications, of substance. In more contemporary terms, instead of using the noun "consciousness" it would be less confusing to employ the word as an adjective.[18] In Cartesian terms this is to say that what there is is not minds and bodies, but mental and physical phenomena. Mind-body dualism is being abandoned. And with it metaphysics overcome. This was hard to see at first, because James was driven by his language to speaking of mental and physical experiences as elements of "pure experience."

Under the influence of the dualist model we tend to regard the physical "world" as real and the mental as not real, or somehow not real. Ideas seem to be ethereal, ghostly "things," and we distinguish the fictional from the real. Real estate becomes a man's real (only, important) property. But James was coming to see that mental phenomena are just as real as the physical.[19] All that distinguishes them is that they have different relations to each other. Physical things are so related that they can have size. And so James could see that God *does* exist. He has influenced the lives of countless numbers of people. That you want to say, "It is the *idea* of God that exists," only shows the hold of the dualist outlook.

James was approaching the realization that each part of experience is equally valuable, *or* that each part has no value. And this is to see, since there are values, we do evaluate, that we put values into experience. They are our creatures. Things have value because they are valued. Valuings are also elements of pure experience, but they are the results of our doing.[20]

By this means one can see a relation between James and Zen Buddhism. The Zen Buddhist speaks of detachment. When it is seen that things do not have value, but that they are valued, detachment is understandable. If things do not have value, then we do not *have* to value them. We can, therefore, become detached from them, take them or leave them. All that is required, and it sounds trite in the saying, though it needs much in the understanding—all that is required is self-control. And this can come with self-awareness.

The impression grows strong here that metaphysics and logic are ways of coming to a knowledge of the self. It has seemed that they were sciences like the natural sciences and that in doing them things were found out about the world. It now seems that they have this other role, provided that they are not played as games.

Let us return to the difficulty into which James seemed to get himself in the matter of God's existence. He said that believing that God exists makes a difference, and that if you want to believe it, this makes the belief true. In other words, God exists because some people believe that he does. It now appears that what looks like confusion here can be explained by seeing that James was getting toward the notion that concepts and theories are instruments and not mirrors of the structure of reality. It looks as though he were wrong, until one sees that James underwent a philosophical development.

An interest in religion was followed, in his thought, by the idea of the will to believe, with the attendant apparent confusion about the matter of God's existence. In the attempt to deal with this difficulty James moved on to see that philosophical inclinations are largely a matter of temperament, and to the talk of pragmatism. This led to a theory of truth and to one of cognition, and these in turn to the analysis of consciousness and to radical empiricism. It is not so much that "an idea is true if you want it to be" as that concepts are instruments. No questions about reality are involved here. It is rather that one is moving to a different slant on concepts. And the important thing to note about concepts is their workability or lack of it. As long as we harp on their truth or falsity (old-style) we are stuck with the dualistic model. The notion of the will to believe is a step on the way to the notion that concepts are instruments, although it sounds all wrong when taken with the dualist model in the background of the mind.

Concepts, then, do not tell us what reality is in the manner in which a photograph informs us about a person. They enable us to predict. The connection between this instrumentalism and the "theory" about consciousness may be seen when one realizes that both work in the direction of destroying the hold which the dualistic model has on us. It is as though theories about concepts and consciousness are not important. What is important is the shifting of models and the possibility this opens up of not being attached to any one model.

The outcome is mysticism, or the state of mind in which one realizes that there is no such thing as a *conceptual* understanding of the world. What is reality? Looked at in one way, this question has no answer. The logical positivists were right with their doctrine of meaningless questions. Perhaps if James had had this equipment he would have been able to go further *in making himself clear*. (Note the ambiguity: making his self clear.) However, looked at in another way, the question has a simple and obvious answer. What is reality? Live it. Live. But reality is ineffable. It cannot be put into words. Clearly, therefore, words, concepts, do not mirror reality. It is obvious that they are not pictures. And to see that they are instruments is to see this. But one cannot see it from the standpoint of the dualist base. And mysticism seems mysterious, instead of common sense, on the basis of the dualist model.

Contemporary philosophy a reaction against idealism? A seeing through it? Rather a move to mysticism.

Logical Positivism   These matters have been approached by another route. In Europe in the mid-nineteenth century, Comte said that the only knowledge is science, positive knowledge. Religion and metaphysics seem to explain the world, the one in terms of personal forces, the other in terms of impersonal forces. But they do not enable us to make predictions. They are, he might have said, as Freud did later, illusions.

At the turn of the century in Vienna, Ernst Mach became more detailed in his positivism. He pointed out that the physical sciences were shot through with metaphysical concepts, or concepts which "refer to" hidden or nonobservable forces. The sciences should be rid of these. Genuine concepts, he thought, are simply economical devices for summarizing experiences in order to enable us to make predictions.[21]

In 1929 the members of the so-called Vienna Circle, influenced by Wittgenstein's *Tractatus Logico-Philosophicus,* announced a program in philosophy: (*a*) to provide a secure foundation for the sciences, (b) to demonstrate the meaning-lessness of all metaphysics by (c) the logical analysis of propositions and concepts. The group had two fundamental doctrines. The first was that statements which purport to say something about the world can be tested only in experience. The second was that this empirical reference can be conclusively shown by logical analysis; that is, by analyzing propositions into their constituents by logical techniques. It turned out that when this was done there would be nothing left to "philosophy" but the analysis of concepts.[22]

To carry out their program the positivists, and notably Rudolph Carnap, employed and developed many of the techniques of symbolic logic. For example, in Aristotelian logic propositions or statements had been analyzed into the subject-predicate form. *Paul is tall* serves as a paradigm. *Paul,* the subject, is connected by *is,* the copula, to the predicate *tall.* This form was represented notationally by *S-P.* General statements such as *All men are mortal* have the same form. They simply refer to some or all of the members of a class.

A different analysis of statements is provided in symbolic logic. An examination of *Paul is tall* and *All men are mortal* suggests that they do or should have the same logical form. Thus, *Paul is tall* attributes a property to an individual, whereas *All men are mortal* says that one class of beings (men) is included in another class (the mortals). Furthermore, *Paul is tall* would be false if there were no men, but *All men are mortal* could be true (if men did exist, then they would be mortal). These differences can be taken into account by introducing the notion of propositional functions.

By analogy with mathematical functions a proposition or statement may be regarded as a function. If we suppose that there are individual things and that they have properties, in statements about them the symbol representing the property may be taken as a function of the symbol standing for the individual. If we formalize our notation completely so that we have no symbols in it referring either to individuals or properties we obtain a way of representing the form of a proposition. Thus $B(x)$ represents *Paul is tall*. You get *Paul is tall* by replacing the variable x by *Paul* and the variable B by *tall*. A propositional function yields a proposition when operations like this are performed on it.

Suppose, further, that other operations can be performed on a propositional function to obtain a proposition. For example, we could generalize it, employing the symbol (x) which reads *for all x's* and get $(x).B(x)$. Substituting *tall* for B, $(x).B(x)$ says *everything is tall*. Or we could specialize $B(x)$, as by the symbol $(\exists x)$, which reads *for some x's*, and obtain $(Ex).B(x)$ which says *some things are tall*.

Turning back to the analysis of *All men are mortal* we find that this proposition may be regarded as though it said something about two properties, being human and being mortal. It says that *if something is human, then it is mortal*. That is, $H(x)$ implies $M(x)$, or more completely $(x).H(x)$ implies $M(x)$: for everything whatsoever, if it is human then it is mortal. $(x).H(x)$ *implies* $M(x)$ is clearly different in form from $B(x)$, and both show that *All men are mortal* has a different logical form from that of *Paul is tall*.

Furthermore, this analysis reveals that the words in a statement can be classified into logical words (*for everything, for some things, implies*), proper names (*Paul*) and adjectives (*mortal, human*, etc.). To put the matter otherwise, logical analysis shows that we can dispense with all common nouns and still say whatever we would want to say. (Accustomed as we are to the subject-predicate sentence, speaking this way would be cumbersome at first. The point is that it could be done.)

The vital bearing of this lugubrious formal analysis of propositions is seen when it is compared with James' analysis of consciousness. The latter, as we have noticed, can be interpreted as issuing in the recommendation that we use the adjective "conscious" rather than the noun "consciousness." The symbolic logician has done in a general way what James was doing in a particular way. He has shown that we can always so express ourselves, except when referring to some particular person or thing, as never to employ words that refer to things. We can, that is, express ourselves, "talk about" the world, without referring to what philosophers have called substances.

This enables us to see the family resemblance between James and the positivists (*and* the logicians), and gives additional insight into the wellsprings of James' thought. He was an empiricist. That is, he believed that knowledge is connected with experience. This led him to be wary about concepts which seemed to refer to things which could not be experienced. Thus, it is impossible to see consciousness, although one can see conscious behavior. And it is impossible to see matter, although one can see material objects: wooden ones, yellow ones, and so on. The resemblance between James and the positivists lies in their empiricism and their movement away from metaphysics. And it tells us that the positivists were also moving away from dualism, although they did not talk that way.

In the literature of Zen Buddhism there is an anecdote of a master who handed a fan to a disciple, asking, "What is this?" The disciple handed it back and said, "A fan." The master frowned in disapproval and handed the fan to a second disciple with the same question. Without a word, the disciple took the fan, scratched his back with it, opened it, fanned himself, closed it, pointed with it, and opening it, placed a flower on it and handed it back to the master. The latter smiled in approval.

James and the formal analysis of propositions suggest the

possibility that nouns have uses but not meaning, that is, that they do not refer to anything. This suggests the further possibility of not regarding what we ordinarily call a thing as a thing. That is to say, we can come to regard things as not being fixed in kind as we ordinarily take them to be, as not having essences. The fan can be used as a back-scratcher. The mountain raises you into the air; you do not climb it. In the language of the Buddhists, things can be seen to be egoless.

It is curious that the formal analysis of propositions should have such profound philosophical bearings and that it should even lay bare a relation between Western and Eastern thought. Perhaps this curiosness is due simply to the use we make of such analyses. In any event, there is yet another device of the logicians which has such bearings.

This is Russell's tool for dealing with the vicious-circle paradoxes. These have latterly been a sore trial to mathematicians, but they have been generally known for a long time. One of them is the paradox of the liar. If a Cretan says, "All Cretans are liars," and we ask whether his statement is true (is he a liar?), we see the paradox. For if his statement is true, then it is false.

Russell "solved" the paradox by noting that it does not appear if we establish a rule that a statement about a class of statements is not itself a member of that class. This rule is reasonable if we suppose that there is a hierarchy of languages; that is, that there can be statements about statements, and statements about those, and so on. Thus, the Cretan's statement is about things that Cretans say and the rule prevents its application to itself. It takes *All Cretans are liars* out of the class of statements made by Cretans.

But it *is* a statement by a Cretan, and therefore the rule is even more arbitrary than rules usually are? However, consider the fact that the notion of a hierarchy of languages is well substantiated in common linguistic usage. If I say, "Boston is north of New York," I am talking about Boston. When I say, "Boston has six letters," I am not; I am talking about the word Boston. And in most courses in a foreign language we use our own language to talk about the foreign one. In the context no device is needed to show this. When language is written we use quotation marks to make it apparent. Thus, in its written form the statement that Boston has six letters would appear as: "Boston" has six letters.

Employing Wittgenstein's theory of meaning in the *Tractatus,* Carnap turned these seemingly trivial considerations into a powerful philosophical device.[23] He distinguished between what he called the material and the formal modes of speech. Roughly put, this is the distinction between language which is about things (at least, non-linguistic things) and language which is about language. When statements about language are mistakenly taken to be about things we get results which cannot be verified, and which must therefore be meaningless even though they seem to make sense. When, however, such statements are "translated" into the formal mode of speech they turn out to be verifiable. Or, if they cannot be so translated they must be regarded as meaningless. Carnap came to think that philosophical propositions are of this sort. He classified them as being in the pseudo-material mode.

The ancient philosophical problem of identity is a simple example. Plato raised it by asking, "Is this the same Socrates sitting here now who walked in the market place yesterday?" Since his properties have changed, how can he be the same? Is the baby, Paul Wienpahl, the same person as the one writing this sentence? A prominent solution to this problem has been given by invoking the concept of the soul. Yes, it is the same person for, though his properties have changed, his soul has not. (Souls are by nature unchanging. This is a philosophical

24

reason for belief in the immortality of the soul.) But who has seen a soul? How can you verify empirically that there are souls, or better, that they are immortal?

If we suppose, however, that Plato's question was not about Socrates (i.e., in the material mode), but about the word "same" —that it is (when not mis-taken) something like *How do we use the word "same"?*—then the question is easily answered by observation. And, of course, the results of such observation will be empirically verifiable. Centuries of muddleheadedness, as Russell remarked about his theory of descriptions, are hereby cleared up. Nor, as at first seemed, does this mean that philosophers have been some kind of fools and that the history of philosophy is worthless. For Plato's question, though long mistaken, was the beginning of the awareness of langauge, which as far as I am concerned is on the way to the awareness of self (of the subjective as distinct from the objective).[24]

Another example of the positivists' conquest of metaphysics is Carnap's treatment of Heidegger's essay, "What Is Metaphysics?" In answering this question, Heidegger concluded that metaphysics deals with the Nothing. Beyond science, he reasoned, there is nothing. And what of this nothing? This is what the metaphysician must be asking. What does the nothing do? The Nothing nothings—

Schwärmerei, Scheitzerei, Carnap might have muttered. Here is a prize piece of meaninglessness. When we translate statements involving the word *nothing* into logically correct language we see through what is going on in Heidegger. Thus, if I say that nothing is outside and if I want to avoid nonsense, I should put the statement into the formal mode of speech. What I am saying in effect is that the statement *There is something outside is not true.* This makes clear the fact, which for some reason has been overlooked, that *nothing* is not a noun, logically speaking. It is a variation of the device for negating statements, the word *not*. Heidegger's presumably profound musings stem from a logical howler. When they are translated they amount to saying that there is no such study as metaphysics. Another locution puts it that metaphysics is concerned with nothing.

Existentialism   There is disagreement about classifying people as existentialists. Martin Heidegger himself denies that he is one. If, however, you regard existentialism as a move away from metaphysics toward existence, as a distrust of theories and an interest in human experience, then Heidegger is an existentialist. In a way, of course, this would lead to classifying the pragmatists and the positivists as existentialists. But although they moved away from metaphysics, these men—except possibly James—did not then turn to what Heidegger turned to. And that turn is what might justify calling him an existentialist and the others not. In any case I take him as an example.

Compared to the positivists, certainly, Heidegger seems muddleheaded. I do not think that this is characteristic of existentialism. It is rather a mark of the expression of anything new so long as it is new. No, it is the turn Heidegger made after he *conquered* metaphysics that is characteristic of the existential move.

Making the turn was extraordinarily laborious. You have only to read "What Is Metaphysics?" to feel this. And its outcome is still shrouded in mystery. It may even be ineffable. By now, however, we can talk quite simply about the turn. Heidegger himself did, writing twenty years after "What Is Metaphysics?" in an essay called "The Way Back into the Ground of Metaphysics."[25]

Despite Carnap's apparently devastating attack on Heidegger, and yet showing how curiously correct the former was, in 1933 Heidegger wrote of his turn that his "line of thought follows to all appearances the road of metaphysics but at the same time as regards its decisive steps . . . it effects a change in the direction of the inquiry, a change which properly belongs to the *conquest (Überwindung)* of metaphysics." Even Carnap's word "conquest" was used by Heidegger in describing his work, which possibly shows how little philosophers listen to each other.[26]

Earlier he had said that metaphysics deals with nothing, with the Nothing. And he had said that this may be just "cross-talk," which might degenerate into "an empty wrangling about words." However, he continued by saying that if we stick to "logic" we cannot deal with Nothing. "Because we continually meet with failure as soon as we try to turn Nothing into a subject, our inquiry into Nothing is already at an end—always assuming, of course, that reason is the means and thinking the way to an original comprehension of Nothing and its possible revelation." He then paid due homage to logic and plunged into Nothing.

In "What Is Metaphysics?" there ensued dread, awfulness, and "what-is" and "what-is-in-totality" and Nothing. In a postscript to the essay written fourteen years later, Heidegger said, "The question 'What is Metaphysics?' asks a question that goes beyond metaphysics. It arises from a way of thinking which has already entered into the overcoming *(Überwindung)* of metaphysics." He added that this way of thinking is difficult because it is forced to use the language of precisely that which it is trying to overcome. "A *picture* held us captive. And we could not get outside it, for it lay in our language and language seemed to repeat it to us inexorably" *(Philosophical Investigations,* No. 115).

All the talk of nothing turned out to be a pointer—to something about which, six years later, Heidegger could be much clearer with a metaphor, the old metaphor that Descartes used,

27

the tree of knowledge. His purpose, said Heidegger, was to get beyond the tree's roots to the ground itself. And ". . . in so far as a thinker sets out to experience the ground of metaphysics—to recall the truth of Being itself instead of merely representing beings as beings . . . his thinking has in a sense left metaphysics." And ". . . if our thinking should succeed in its efforts to get back into the ground . . . , it might well help to bring about a change in human nature, accompanied by a transformation of metaphysics." "Metaphysics seems almost to be, without knowing it, the barrier which keeps man from the original involvement of Being in human nature." ". . . every philosophy which revolves around an indirect or a direct conception of 'transcendence' remains of necessity an ontology, whether it achieves a new foundation of ontology or whether it assures us that it repudiates ontology as a conceptual freezing of experience." We need ". . . to prepare the transition from representational thinking to a new kind of thinking." That is why he asked, What is metaphysics? However, little can be done ". . . before every attempt is made to liberate the determination of human nature from the concept of subjectivity and from the concept of the *animale rationale.*"

To put it baldly, I think that Heidegger was turning to mysticism. That is, he was turning to a way of knowing, or an awareness experience, in which ideas and theories play no part. This is why he came to believe that the conquest of metaphysics led to a concern with Nothing. It led to a concern with what cannot be put into words—or, when it is, is lost ("the conceptual freezing of experience"). Dewey got through metaphysics and turned to practical problems (education, social issues). Carnap conquered metaphysics and turned to the logical analysis of the concepts of science. Sartre took up phenomenological analyses of ethics and psychoanalysis. Possibly James was moving in the same direction as Heidegger. He dealt sympathetically with mysticism in *The Varieties of Religious Experience*. However, we need not decide this.

Since the conquest of metaphysics is the abandonment of dualism, it can lead to foreseeing a kind of conscious experience in which there is no distinction between subject and object. Heidegger seems to have done this. Whether he had such experiences is another question, one that only he can answer.

It is as though there were now in philosophy various methods or ways: logical analysis, examinations of the ideas of truth and cognition, Wittgenstein's. The outcome of these ways has been to turn men back to experience. In so far as the theoretical and the intellectual had become everything for the Westerner, the outcome is to turn them to nothing. The encounter with Nothing is a confrontation with no-metaphysics. It is equivalent to seeing through the parent (God). It leaves men without value.

Wittgenstein   The most recent of these ways in philosophy is Ludwig Wittgenstein's. It lies through the keep of the castle of philosophy, which is logic, and issues in a new and powerful technique of analysis. This technique has so dazzled people that they have mistaken it for the substance of Wittgenstein's work. However, the technique *is* finally all, and its employment results in no arguments or theories. Thus, Wittgenstein's work can only be described if the technique is not illustrated in a special analysis.[27]

In Plato's *Phaedo* Socrates asks a question: Do you believe in beauty, in justice? The answer is yes. But did you ever behold them with your eyes? Or any other bodily sense? No, I've only seen beautiful things. And is not the same true of greatness, health, strength, or the essence of anything? Is it not solely by intellectual vision that we have the conception of essences?

The existence of concepts or general ideas has constituted a problem ever since Plato. Where do they come from? We *see* only particulars or individual things, never general ones. Yet we can think of the latter. In fact this is the nature of thought: it seems to deal with what is general or universal.

Until recently there have been two solutions to the problem.[28] Both of them come to Platonism. Plato suggested that things have the forms they do because there are Forms (Ideas) by which the things are somehow made. We have ideas of these Forms because we have "seen" them in a previous existence.

The other solution, the empiricist, maintains that we obtain concepts by generalizing from observations of particular things. When it is asked how generalization works, the answer inevitably seems to be: because the things subsumed under a generalization have something in common. They resemble each other. This gets us back to Plato's Forms, although by an obscure path. Thus, the existence of thought seems to require a belief in entities which are not experienced by the senses, and a belief in an agency of some kind different from the bodily senses which apprehends these entities. This agent is the mind.

Wittgenstein came across the issue raised by Socrates' question in a question of his own. What is the nature of a proposition? How can there be false propositions? The answer seemed to require a notion of "things," not observable by the senses, to which these propositions refer. We can say, for example, that a true proposition refers to an actual state of affairs (*Snow is white* because snow is white). However, what happens when the state of affairs no longer exists and what is the state of affairs to which *Snow is not white* refers?

Wittgenstein initially solved his problem in the *Tractatus* by constructing a theory of language, or rather giving precise form to one proposed by Aristotle and taken for granted ever since. According to this theory, words, and particularly nouns, are the building blocks of language. They are language's connection with things. They have the naming relation to things. With them propositions (sentences) are formed. However, sentences do not refer to anything. They do not, as we commonly suppose, mean anything.

With this Wittgenstein gets the answer to his problem. Words have meaning. Sentences do not. Therefore, the problem of what a false proposition refers to is solved. Wittgenstein solved the further problem—Why are propositions significant if they do not have meaning?—by supposing that they have a *sense,* something like a direction. True propositions are those whose sense corresponds to that of a state of affairs. The sense of false propositions does not so correspond. A proposition is like a picture. It either corresponds (resembles) or does not correspond to what it supposedly depicts. We construct false propositions, at least of one kind, by the use of the word *not.* We might as well invert them. Thus again, the question of what a false proposition refers to disappears. We are hereby rid of one need to believe in nonempirical entities.

However, Wittgenstein came to see that the picture theory of language will not do. There is something deeply wrong with it. For it simply shifts his problem from the nature of the meaning of propositions to one about the meaning of words, notably nouns. We can see how proper names refer or are related to things. They are like tags. But what about common or general nouns? *Cats* refers to cats. But what about all the dead-and-gone cats and those to come? Moreover, the word *cat* does not refer to a particular cat. And for that matter, what about the proper name *Paul* when Paul is dead? How is it like a tag on a box? How can a tag be a tag when it is tagging nothing? (Wittgenstein once asked, Can you play chess without the queen?)

With this the profundity of Wittgenstein's problem began to appear. No analysis of the sort he performed with propositions was going to work any longer. He found himself faced with what he came to call the "civil status" of a contradiction. How can there be a word (a noun) which is not a word—that is, which does not mean anything?

Gradually it becomes clear that this question reaches down into the depths of our rational being. It is about our very relation to, our place in, our world. For with it we see that language seems inexplicable without the supposition that there are minds, intellects, which are different from all other things in that they have some connection with the general, the abstract, the non-concrete. The problem of the relation of language to the world is, in other words, the mind-body problem in a particular form.

The nature of the problem, its likeness to being confronted by a contradiction, and its profundity, indicate that logic will not solve it. It is about the mind itself. The situation resembles that which confronts the psychoanalyst. We have to go beneath the surface. We seem to be confronted with an illness rather than a problem. And Wittgenstein did employ the medical metaphor. There is not a method in philosophy, he said, but rather methods, like different therapies.[29]

Thus, as he lectured at Cambridge in the 1930's, Wittgenstein was not so much teaching as he was talking to himself. And the *Philosophical Investigations* which came out of this is often a dialogue between the Wittgenstein of the *Tractatus* and of the *Investigations*. Further, he went beyond logic in the sense that the *Investigations* is not an essay. It is ostensibly about language, but does not provide us with a theory of language. It is seemingly not a connected discourse. It is rather a collection of examples, and the relations between them are psychological, not logical. Its style is clear, firm, and simple. But it is devilishly hard to read, and almost impossible to teach.

The function of these examples is to jolt us into taking a brisk look at matters which we have taken for granted—in this case our ordinary view of how language works. We think it works because words have meaning. How do you obey the order, bring me a yellow flower? Because you know what yellow means. You have a mental image of yellow which enables you to recognize a *yellow* flower. But how, then, do you obey the order, *imagine* a yellow patch? You seem to do so automatically. And so Wittgenstein was to repeat, "Don't look for the meaning, look for the use."

I shall not illustrate further the method of the *Investigations*. It is original. It is Wittgenstein's. It is there for any to read. I am here only concerned with the material on which it is used. This is, it seems to me, the mind-body problem and dualism in all its forms, though Wittgenstein only mentions the former and apparently ignores the latter.

The *Investigations* has dazzled us with its style. Its real appeal, however, is the way it gets down into us and amongst us so deeply that it does not need—nor was it given—any statement of its plan.

Wittgenstein spoke of the outcome of his work. It was to be "complete clarity." And "this simply means that the philosophical problems should *completely* disappear." "The real discovery is the one that makes me capable of stopping doing philosophy when I want to. —The one that gives philosophy peace. . . ." Some will say that he meant clarity about language. But when the deeper implications of his work are taken into account I find that he meant more. "Stopping doing philosophy," "the real discovery," and bringing "light into one brain or another . . . in the darkness of this time" show this.

They also show that dualism engenders metaphysics, or, as he called it, philosophy. Complete clarity comes when mind-body dualism is dissolved. And Wittgenstein was right. Dualism is not objective. It is subjective. It is an illness, an illusion; a "superstition (*not* a mistake!)." What is needed are different

33

"therapies." *We,* not the world or language, have to be straightened out. The problem is a spiritual one.

The cloud of unknowing. "What is your aim in philosophy? —To shew the fly the way out of the fly-bottle." On his deathbed: "Tell them I've had a wonderful life."[30]

NOTES

1. This chapter is written in a style of thought I had before the events reported in what follows. Today I would say "Western men." Western men tend to use the term man to refer only to Westerners.

2. Descartes assumed that knowledge is like a mathematical system: for example, Euclidean geometry with the axioms and theorems. It is composed of basic propositions and all those that can be deduced from them. Therefore, he had only to find the basic propositions to allay his doubts.

3. And thus were values removed from the "world" and the development of psychology retarded till the twentieth century. Whatever its biological worth, rat "psychology" is not a science of the human psyche. Outside of novels, not until Freud did we have anything like that.

4. James wrote in a letter in 1903: "I have got my mind working on the infernal old problem of mind and brain, and how to construct the world out of pure experiences, and feel foiled again and inwardly sick with the fever. But I verily believe that it is only work that makes one sick in that way that has any chance of breaking old shells and getting a step ahead. It is a sort of madness however when it is on you. The total result is to make me admire "Common Sense" as having done by far the biggest stroke of genius ever made in philosophy when it reduced the chaos of crude experience by its luminous *Denkmittel* of the stable "thing," and its dualism of thought and matter." *Letters of William James,* Henry James, ed. (Boston: *Atlantic Monthly Press,* 1920), Vol. II, p. 198.

Talking about his work, Wittgenstein once said, "At first sight it may appear (but why it should can only become clear later) that we have two kinds of worlds, worlds built of different materials, a mental world and a physical world." The mental world seems ethereal, and we are embarrassed about this, but the grammar of certain words seems to make it necessary. "This is a hint as to how the problem of the two materials, *mind* and *matter,* is going to be solved." Ludwig Wittgenstein, *The Blue and Brown Books,* (Oxford: Basil Blackwell, 1960), p. 47.

I have left Spinoza out of this. He solved the problem but was not listened to.

5. Locke's important conclusion that ideas come from experience resulted from his belief that they could have only one other possible origin: they are innate, in our minds at birth, placed there perhaps, as Descartes thought, by God. Since this view is preposterous on a number of grounds, Locke thought the other must be the correct one.

Especially when laid out at length this kind of thinking appears enormously abstract and impractical. It has thus made people regard philosophers as peculiar. That it has, however, vital connections with our daily lives may be seen as follows. If knowledge is limited to experience, then each person must be tolerant of another's beliefs, for the other may have had experiences which justify his views. This consideration led Locke to the principle of political democracy. The totalitarian, on the other hand, has always had to claim that he had some special pipeline to knowledge which was denied to others.

6. Lest some begin to read this with dismay, let me point out that I am not writing a history of modern philosophy. I am making my sketch of the picture which Wittgenstein said has "held us captive." Nor should we confuse experience with our picture of it.

7. Consider, for example, the view that the world had a beginning in time, was created. This means that there was a time when the world was not. But is not time a part of reality? (Time unreal?) Furthermore, this contradictory character of the view about the beginnings of the world helps to explain the fact that some people

have thought the world had a beginning in time and others that it did not. They could thus hold opposite views because the views are impossible; that is, meaningless or without cogency.

8. That there is, as William James was to say, simply experience. No world and experience *of* it; simply "pure experience" in which one of our activities is the establishment of control. In seeing this one finds that the problem of truth goes by the board. It is replaced by the question: Does this work?

Biologists say that ontogeny recapitulates phylogeny. In his biological development the human being recapitulates the evolutionary development of the animal world. It is almost as though we could speak of the same thing at work in the spiritual development of a person. He recapitulates human history. The view that we come into a ready-made world is the view of the child. With it we easily believe in the great counterpart of our own human fathers. In this stage of our development we take no responsibility for our actions and at first have none. Gradually maturation changes this—to a greater or less degree, until Sartre was able to say that he is responsible for everything that any human being does. However, his insight is not new. St. Augustine had it in his conception of a God who performed his wonders without knowledge of good and evil (for that would have limited his freedom, his will). The language is different, the insight into the human soul the same. Augustine was simply not bothered by the subject-object distinction, and therefore could talk of himself by talking of God.

In "Existentialism as a Humanism" Sartre denies that he is an atheist. He has, he says, simply worked out the consequences of supposing that God does not exist.

9. The pre-Socratics, Augustine, and the neo-Platonists. However, these roots can be seen in Plato as well, when he is read as being more mystical than our rational tradition would have him.

There were, of course, a host of other factors which influenced the profound change that is going on here, for example, the Industrial

36

Revolution. It must be impossible to think as men did before that event.

10. Hegel said that only one man understood him and that was Hegel. A reviewer of Stirling's *The Secret of Hegel* wrote simply that the secret was well kept. It may seem to us now that even Hegel was a blind seer. Notice that, although I am talking about Hegel and refer to "we" and "us," I am concerned with myself.

11. In his autobiography in the "Library of Living Philosophers", Vol. 5. Evanston: The Library of Living Philosophers, Inc., 1946, p. 12. Russell was to describe the joy he experienced in 1900 when, coming out from the influence of Hegelianism, he again saw the trees as trees and the grass as really green.

12. I found later that this *confusion* of the subjective with the objective is enormously important when it is rather a *mingling*. As noted, William James struggled to get beyond the distinction, although he realized that it was the most ingenious of the inventions of common sense.

13. In the first issue, in the year 1900, of the influential British journal of philosophy and psychology, *Mind,* there appeared a picture titled "The Absolute in the Pink of Condition." It was a blank pink sheet. There followed articles such as "The Disappearance of Reality."

14. Interestingly, Dewey remarked that this move could have occurred when the development of modern science first appeared in the 1500's. And as I read Spinoza, he made it, though not for the reasons Dewey did. That is, Spinoza abandoned the distinctions (such as God and the world, mind and body, good and evil). He was not widely read in his day. However, we can now see his kinship to Dewey and James.

15. I wanted to say "clarify it." However, Dewey was a careless writer and many would say that the last thing he does is to clarify. James, on the other hand, was a fine writer, and some would say that his fire also gives off more smoke than light. It seems, rather,

that anything new is difficult of expression. At first we have only
the old words for it. This is particularly the case when the new is
profoundly revolutionary and at the same time goes to the core of
all our beliefs and attitudes.

16. Cf. Wittgenstein, who remarks in *The Blue Book* that *the*
problem is the mind-body issue. Then in the Preface to *philosophical
Investigations* he says that "it is not impossible that it should fall
to the lot of this work, in its poverty and in the darkness of this time,
to bring light into one brain or another—but, of course, it is not
likely" (Oxford: Basil Blackwell, 1953). Wittgenstein is regarded by
some as the father of linguistic philosophy. If he is, his progeny seem
to have moved far from his central concern.

Heidegger—let us then go beyond logic if it won't do.

17. Though it may not be needed in 1970. The times are changing
so rapidly that the young may no longer be caught up in dualism.
Still, as Wittgenstein said, "A *picture* held us captive. And we could
not get outside it, for it lay in our languages and languages seemed
to repeat it to us inexorably." *Investigations,* No. 115.

18. Although Spinoza's terms "substance" and "modes" imply
this, he explicitly speaks of it in the "Essay on the Improvement
of the Understanding," (*Spinoza's Works* (New York: Dover
Publications, 1951), Vol. II, p. 36. Definitions of uncreated things (a
substance) "must contain, as far as the mind is concerned, no substan-
tives which could be put into an adjectival form; in other words, the
object defined must not be explained through abstractions." This is
to say that substances must be referred to only by proper names. See
below, p. 21.

Cf. Wittgenstein's: "We make the mistake of looking for a substance wherever there is a substantive" (*The Blue and Brown Book*,
p. 1). The actual quotation is: "We are up against one of the greatest
sources of philosophical bewilderment: a substantive makes us look
for a thing that corresponds to it." From this one sees that Spinoza's
substance is not that of which experience is made or which causes it.

It *is* experience, just as the referents of proper names are matters of experience. Such a view is not monism. It is nondualism. The word "monism" implies a theory.

19. In "Does Consciousness Exist?" he called attention to "weighty" ideas. In the Middle Ages men thought in terms of degrees of reality. Some things were regarded as more real than others; the Church, for example, was more real than any one of its individual members. This way of thinking justified the Inquisition. It later justified Hitler. It is understandable when you notice that the word "real" is ambiguous. To say a thing is real is to say that it exists. It is also sometimes to say that it is important. "Real" is sometimes a value word.

20. Dewey concludes *Experience and Nature* with a chapter in which he equates facts and values and speaks of a science of values. Spinoza said that there is no good and evil. There are only what men call good and evil. For the logical positivists value terms simply express emotions.

21. Thinking along these lines led Mach to claim that only sensations are real, which brought charges of subjectivism. It is, however, James' notion of pure experience in another form, another example of how hard it is to overcome dualism.

22. Perhaps because of his work in logic, the logical positivists traced their antecedents to Leibnitz. It is clear, however, that their work has been very like David Hume's. He did not use the apparatus of the formal logician, but he did analyze ideas and try to trace them to their origins in experience. By this means he concluded that many of our ideas are "vacuous." In fact, of course, this skepticism goes back to Protagoras and the Greek Skeptic, Pyrrho.

Why be pedantic? Only to indicate how deeply our spiritual roots and our troubles go.

23. Wittgenstein had distinguished between the meaning and the truth of a proposition. Its meaning is its method of verification. C. S. Peirce had done the same sort of thing. The distinction provided a

theory of meaning, and revealed as important a kind of proposition to which little attention had been paid, although it was well known. According to the theory a proposition is meaningful if it is veriable as true or false. Otherwise it is meaningless. We all know of "statements" like " 'Twas brillig and the slithy toves did gyre and gimbal in the wabe," which are obviously nonsense or meaningless. This theory of meaning, however, makes it possible to see that there are sentences which are grammatically correct but may be considered logically meaningless. Take, for example, "the world doubled in size last night." How would you verify the statement? Measure your table? But the ruler has doubled in size. Thus, according to the verifiability theory of meaning, the statement is meaningless although it is grammatically sound. Cf. "How many hairs must a man lose to become bald?"

24. Wittgenstein wondered in the *Philosophical Investigations* why his investigations seemed only "to destroy everything interesting, that is, all that is great and important" (No. 118). And remember James on that handy *Denkmittel* of common sense: the distinction between "thought-stuff" and "think-stuff." Carnap's analysis of Heidegger, which follows, is in the former's "Uberwindung der Metaphysic durch Logische Analyse der Sprache," Erkenntnis (Spring, 1931).

25. "What Is Metaphysics?" was first a lecture. It appeared as an essay in English in his *Existence and Being* (Chicago: Henry Regnery & Co., 1949). The other essay is in *Existentialism from Dostoevsky to Sartre,* Walter Kaufmann, ed. (New York: Meridian Books, 1957). The details of this section and Carnap's analysis may be found in P. Wienpahl, "Philosophy and Nothing," *Chicago Review* (Summer, 1959).

26. During 1930-33 Wittgenstein told Moore that there was now a "kink in the development of human thought" and that he was doing a "new subject" and not merely on a stage in "a continuous development." (*Mind,* No. 253 [Jan., 1955]). The quotation is from M.

Heidegger, "On the Essence of Truth," in *Existence and Being,* p. 351.

27. There is a fuller discussion of this view of Wittgenstein by the present writer in the journal *Inquiry*: "Wittgenstein and the Naming Relation" Vol. 7, No. 4 (1964); "Wittgenstein's Notebooks 1914-1916," (1969); and "The Tractatus," (1970).

28. A new solution is the pragmatists': we invest concepts. We do not discover them. There was this much truth in the theory of innate ideas.

29. *Investigations,* No. 133. This metaphor is common in the literature of Far Eastern mystics, which Wittgenstein, so far as I know, never read. Lin Chi (Rinzai) in ninth-century China compared his teaching to the doctor's art. And Wang Yang-ming in the sixteenth century, when accused of contradicting himself with his different teachings, replied that he used different pills for different illnesses.

Cf. the letter of William James quoted in n. 4 above.

30. Quotations in the preceding three paragraphs from *Philosophical Investigations,* Preface and Nos. 111, 133, 309; and Norman Malcolm, *Ludwig Wittgenstein, A Memoir,* last page.

CHAPTER TWO

THERE IS ANOTHER ROUTE BY WHICH THE MATTERS AT HAND MAY be approached.[1] It involves an exercise of the mind, as have the preceding courses. However, unlike the approaches mentioned earlier, this one also includes as essential to it a physical exercise and certain other nonintellectual factors. Clearly I cannot bring the physical exercise into this book, although I can give a description of the way it is performed (see Appendix). So I can only urge upon you that the exercise is a vital part of the path. In what follows, one must bear in mind that the phases of this approach of which one learns as one reads must be accompanied by the physical aspect.

On the other hand, I can bring in many of the other nonintellectual factors, and it will be necessary to do so. Therefore this book reads quite unlike the philosophic essays to which we have grown accustomed in the West. As far as I can see, the philosophic route on which I am now embarking differs essentially from those described in Chapter One precisely by reason of all these nonintellectual factors which inevitably go with it. The present method leads toward a dissolution of the mind-body dualism, as well as through the idealist frame of mind. And the presence of nonintellectual factors is not only a part of the method, but itself in a way *represents* the dissolution of dualism.

Sitting quietly, the roshi says, "I am going to give you something to work on, and you'll work on it with this." He points to my stomach. "You must get beyond existence and non-existence, being and non-being.

"Joshu, that is a proper name, was sitting and a monk asked him: Does the dog have Buddha-nature? Joshu's reply was; 'Mu,' which means no. But, said the monk, the Buddha said that all sentient creatures have the Buddha-nature. How can your answer be correct? *Mu!* said Joshu."

1 The roshi continues: "You have to understand that 'mu.' You have to get beyond existence and nonexistence. And you have to do it here!" This time he pokes me in the stomach with his short staff.

Bell.

2 Later that day I commenced work on the koan, both during zazen and as one might work on any problem. Although I believed that the goal was to get free of all thought, various "thoughts" entered my mind (head).[2]

As I see koans now, the following may be involved: There is ratiocinative thinking (scientific, practical). It leads to theories, and hence to control. There is also what may be called intuitive thinking. It leads to consciousness, or a consciousness of a particular thing, in which you let the thing alone. You do not interfere with it, classify it, make plans for it, possess it, and so on. You let it live its own life.

To use rather old-fashioned language, we have faculties both for ratiocinative knowledge and for intuitive knowledge. Both need training. During the work reported in Chapter One, I came to realize that there is such a thing as intuitive knowledge. Koan exercise is a means for developing the faculty for it. There are undoubtedly other ways. But the koan, like everything else, has a life of its own. It will show you things about it if you will let it. The problem is to let it. You cannot solve the koan. Eventually it will "speak" to you. As a flower can. Or a person.

Again, the problem is to get yourself into a position in which the koan, or anything else, can speak, can have its life in your presence. The same goes for people. (Remember how uninterested you are in another's journey when he returns from a trip?)

This is why so-called mysticism does not lead to retirement and otherworldliness. Just the reverse. It leads to fuller participation because, when you have developed the intuitive faculty, there can be more than one person (yourself) in your experience. The mystical person is not so rare as we suppose—at least not quite what we suppose. He is not a man with his head in the clouds. Such people exist, but they are attached to the *idea* of mysticism. So Rinzai says: Stamp on the Buddha, spit on him! Don't, that is, get attached to an idea (for you cannot be attached to the Buddha, since he has been dead for 2,500 years).

That poke in the stomach. Solve the koan not with your head but with the center of your being. It is you who will solve it, not your mind. And that means: let the koan take over, let it speak. The concentration required is not on the koan. It is on yourself. To let go and to let the koan have its own life. The struggle is to let go (Zen Buddhists speak of "the drop into the bottomless abyss"). (Is this why people working on koans see things about themselves?)

Does this take a koan? Would not the learning to let anything speak do the trick? ——And, if you can let others talk, possibly you could let yourself talk.

Now look how my mind wanders. These theories are fine, but what about the koan? Every thought keeps you from it. So you have to work at it and not work at it. Possibly keeping the koan before you and not trying to keep the thoughts out will work (as you do when you count as you breathe during zazen). Clearly the difficulty is with myself and not with the koan. I cannot be myself. The thoughts always take over. If I could be myself I could see the koan as it is.[3]

All right, why *did* Joshu say that the dog does not have

Buddha-nature? To get the monk away from a theory. The monk thought that the dog has Buddha-nature because the Buddha had said so. Joshu says: "Mu!" It is not that the dog either does or does not have Buddha-nature. Also, the monk already knew what the Buddha had said. Why, therefore, did he ask Joshu? He had doubts, say. Or was testing Joshu? Why? Joshu was a recognized master (or enlightened man). So, is Joshu in effect saying: Don't have doubts? And is he in his answer showing his own Buddha-nature (enlightenment)? How?

Much of the above concerning koans comes from reading about them. But is that not all right, to have the words become your own? ——Am I also being misled by so-and-so's claim that a word or two solves a koan? I will keep looking for that word.[4]

G. is right about the statue of Manjusri for which I am looking. Why *not* make my own? It would not be like the original? But what is the original? Some other man's statue. Why copy his? Why not make your own? Wanting to buy an "original" statue is Platonism, a copy of the original. ——And here is another side of Plato's disgust with imitations. It is not expressed in order to praise pure Forms. It is said in praise of originality. How easy it is to misread, or to read in only one way.

See how I go back and forth between the koan and my thoughts? I cannot let the koan speak because I (my thoughts) get in the way. (Notice that "I" is sometimes plural, sometimes singular. For purely grammatical considerations?) Yet I am learning about myself thereby (at least how busy my "mind" is and *what* is in it). So I am solving the koan and not solving it. Shall I tell the roshi tomorrow that my answer to the koan is: I am in the way?

I can see now why it is said that it takes a long time to "solve" a koan (to open one's "eyes"). It seems first to become like a mirror in which you see yourself reflected (I bounce back and

45

forth between the koan and myself). Until the self is clear and familiar you will not see the koan, only reflections. So a self-examination is needed first. So, too, is the "solution" of a koan different from the solution of a mathematical problem.

This suggests that it must be true that no one but you can solve the koan on which you are working. That is, it would do no good to be told the answer, because in a sense you are working on yourself to get the answer. This also shows why sanzen interviews are regarded as private: because (*a*) things might come out which are nobody else's business; and (*b*) what is being worked on is private, and can thus be of no interest to anyone else. Finally, I can see that there is a classical answer (i.e., one and only one) to every koan. If the koan has a life of its own, this must be the case. On the other hand, I cannot see how the answer makes much difference. It seems to be the process of getting it that counts.

Why do I feel so urgent about solving the koan? There is the snare again: Platonism. There is more to life than just life.

"Does the dog have Buddha-nature?" seems to be a different question from "What is the cardinal principle of Buddhism?" (In another koan a teacher was asked this question. He replied: "There is a pine tree in garden." Of this reply I read that it demonstrated the principle and was an expression of it.) How can Joshu's answer be an expression of his Buddha-nature? —— But this is to work logically.

This method of the Zen Buddhists has the advantage of setting you to live with one thing and only one. And because there is no logic to it, because it is not classifiable, you cannot dismiss it. You have to live with the koan and yet you cannot *do* anything with it. Finally you must see it as *it* is. Then the answer will be obvious. Before that, it will not be. Therefore, too, there is no use in being told the answer.

The monk says: Look at the roshi when he talks. Watch

46

everything he does. Yet what will I see but the roshi? Do not look for signs. Do not interpret. Listen. But listen to what? Does not listening involve interpreting? Well doesn't seeing? How then can you *see* things as they are? Aha! Don't give *your* interpretation. Listen, look, yes, but do not project yourself into it.

See? I keep thinking there is a word or two which is the answer. But if the thing is illogical, then there is no answer. "Answer" goes with logic. Well, something that will pop into my mind (sic). But then how will I *show* it? Must be a word and an action together, or a word which is an action. And that is what words are when they are not interpreted.[5]

No, I feel that I am always interfering with the koan. Yet when it is there, when I am just looking at it, all I see is it. No "answer," just it. Why did Joshu say no? If he had said yes, then the monk would have been confirmed in an idea. If no then the monk is puzzled and may get away from ideas to himself and thus to reality. ——But note those *if*'s and *then*'s. Well, what is wrong with them? It is also said that koans are logical when understood. And roshis use *if* and *then* in their lectures.

The question is, what does that "mu" (no) *mean*? It means, finally: Do not get caught up in an idea. You are the Buddha *when* you see that. Does the dog have Buddha-nature? Of course, but so what? ——Now the koan seems to be speaking and not I.

How can I answer with my stomach? Is that not just their way of saying: Don't rationalize? Answer intuitively, as you think. But have I thought this answer: "Do not get caught up in an idea"? Did I not get it from Rinzai and others whom I have read? Not exactly. When I said that I was tired of ideas I gave the answer by myself.[6]

As I see it, "getting beyond existence and nonexistence" = "getting beyond 'existence' and 'nonexistence,' "—beyond words, that is, to reality (the nonverbal). I can appreciate that, but I don't often get in touch with it consciously. (Remember Descartes and the careful attention to an idea?) And I have the feeling that I am not so getting in touch with this koan. I am sure of what "mu" means, how and why he used it. But that, I suspect, is just a verbal answer.

6   Why can't I approach the roshi confidently and say that this is as *I* see it? Because that is precisely what you have: as *you* see it. What of *it*? How is *it*?

The answer, or at least the explanation of the "mu," I have. Now the question is, how to *show* it? Do not doubt the explanation because the answer to a koan is supposed to be a word. That is just what you have read. The only question is, how does it fit with your intuition of emptiness?[7] It fits. It is not that the dog

7   does or does not have a soul. It is your being free of all this. The "mu" helps to do this.

Possibly you do not have to show it. Yet, if the old masters express their enlightenment in their answers, does my answer express mine? Is it not too verbal, too logical? Aha! How would *I* answer the monk who asked about the dog? Would my explanation do?

8   But I see now that a koan should be answered with another expression of enlightenment, not with an explanation. It is true that the roshi asked me for an explanation. What did that "mu" mean? But so does the question of the cardinal principle of Buddhism ask for an explanation.[8] The answer is to give one and not to give one. See? Therefore the real question is: What did that "mu" mean? That question is just like: Does the dog have Buddha-nature? What is the cardinal principle of Buddhism? Etc. So what the roshi did was to ask me a philosophic question. And *in a sense,* I am planning to give him a philosophic answer.

Joshu said "Mu." Rinzai said "Ho." What do I say?

Well, at least I *now* see that what the roshi did was to throw at me either the same question or a similar one (to the monk's). *That* is being given a koan. And that is why koans come from mondos, which are questions and answers—for example, question: Does the dog have Buddha-nature? answer: Mu. To ask what the answer means is to start the cycle again. Now I can see why I might be asked to *show* the roshi. That is what an answer to a question of this sort is. It is an answer because it shows the answer.[9]

Of this, that I now have the question, I am sure. Compare this feeling with the feelings I think I have about the answer.

Now, how would I show the roshi my answer? (Do not be misled by thoughts about a verbal answer.) In a sense this is unfair, for he is enlightened, that is, knows the answer. Thus our relationship is the reverse of that of Joshu and the monk. How can I show him? Do not be misled by the classical answer stuff. Concentrate on showing the roshi.

Now, it must be an answer to the question, that is, to: What is the meaning of "mu"? Do not worry about dogs, Buddha-nature, Joshu, etc. It is between the roshi and me. Just the two of us. ——I am still puzzled by the fact that he must know the answer.

Now, what is the meaning of "mu!"? Or, why did Joshu say no? I want to show the roshi that there both is and is not an answer. (I can see now how one might suddenly think of what one was going to say and how it might be quite brief.)

Ah, a good feeling. I feel now that *I* have to answer. How would *I* show a student? Do not think of what Rinzai did, and Joshu. What would I do? ——Note how I am both closer and not closer, and how long it took just to get to the problem.

What does the "mu" mean? And there is an answer, but it has to be shown, not told. Now put that down in your stomach.

I know what the question is *and* what I have to do. I cannot

49

do it. Of course *you* cannot. That is, your mind cannot—see? But you and the question can. You are trying now to *think* of an answer. "How would I deal with a student?" you think. How? How? But that will not do, because that is exactly what the monk was involved in.

I can actually feel it going down into my guts. Why not let it work, therefore? Why try to work on it? Yet you do in a way have to.

What am I trying to become? Just original.[10]

And now I, the whole of me, work on this day and night, as a painter with a painting or a scientist with a problem. (There is a difference there, but it is not as great as it looks.)[11] There is no use in being told the answer, because enlightenment must come on your own, just as an original painting must. You may copy the teachers for technique (for example, "Do it in your stomach"), but the answer *you* get. And I feel now that I will get it, though I have no inkling of it or what it is.

You do not have to do zazen now to get it. But you do have to keep at the koan. Concentrate all the time, that is, bring your forces together and to bear on it. ——(Note how "concentrate" got a better use there.) (See, too, how talk of faith can come in. I *know* that there is something to get and that I *will* get it. However, I do not know what.)

Notice how the question of cardinal principle, the dog question, and mine all differ and yet are the same. Hence, each koan has a different answer.

How can I answer the question so as to *show* emptiness? As "mu" does! You cannot say "mu" means nothing, for it *is* an answer. If you *tell* a man, "Don't worry," he will. And do not keep thinking of other answers to philosophic questions.

The next day Now I have something from the koan as well as all that stuff from myself. Why it took so long to get, I do not know. It is this. The koan is: A monk asked Joshu whether the dog has Buddha-nature or not. Joshu replied: "Mu!" (No!) The background for the koan is that the Buddha had said that all sentient beings have Buddha-nature. So the roshi asks me: What does that "mu" mean? (Why did Joshu say no, when the Buddha had said yes?)[12]

Well, I am sure that Joshu said no because, if he had said yes, he would simply have confirmed the monk in an idea. And the whole point of "getting" zen (getting to the other shore, in the Buddhist phrase) is to cease to be enslaved by ideas (to cease to be confirmed in them).[13] So Joshu says "No," to jolt the monk and to express his own (Joshu's) Buddha-nature. Hence, what I now know is that *the* question—my koan so to speak— is the roshi's question: What does that "mu" mean? This is another question like the monk's. And both are like philosophical questions or puzzlements. Compare them with the question: What is the cardinal principle of Buddhism? to which the answer was: There is a pine tree in the garden.

An interesting thing about these answers given by Zen Buddhists is that they seem illogical and not answers at all, whereas when you understand them they are seen to be perfect answers. "There is a pine tree in the garden" is an expression of the cardinal principle *in an action* (though in words).

In other words, I have to get the sort of answer Joshu gave. The problem then is: to show (not tell) what the "mu" means. Just any old nonsense will not do. It has got to be nonsense (*i. e., not in words*) which is to the point. And I know now that the answer has to come from me. If you are told the answer and then repeat it to the roshi, it will be a copy and he will know it; since it has not come out of you, it will not fit you.

Solving a koan is like painting a picture. There is the thing out there, to be sure, but the painting, if it is not just a copy, has to come from you. One knows an original because it has the stamp of the artist himself on it. In the same way, the roshi can tell from your answer whether it is yours. And I know now that the thing has to come from me. The roshi may give pointers, as copying pictures in the Louvre to develop his technique gives an artist pointers. But the answer has to be mine. There can be no cheating.

Now it seems to me that the answer to the question: What does the "mu" mean, is *mu*. Yet it does not satisfy. It flows somehow too easily from the koan, is too "logical." There should be a break. Compare: What is the cardinal principle of Buddhism? There is a pine tree in the garden.

"Don't look for the meaning, look for the use." How about *that*! Look how that dictum of Wittgenstein fits in a startling way with Zen Buddhism. It all has in it the getting beyond concepts which have been supposed to be the meanings of words. And there is about it an air of advocacy of action which is typical of Zen Buddhism. The trouble is that it is too logical, it fits too beautifully.

Sitting quietly, the roshi listens.

"A monk asked Joshu, 'Does the dog have Buddha-nature or not?' Joshu replied: 'Mu!' What does that 'mu' mean? The 'mu' means: Don't look for the meaning, look for the use."[14]

The roshi smiles and says, as though I had said nothing, "You have got to transcend existence and nonexistence. A equals *b* and *b* equals *c,* then *a* equals *c* is logic. You have got to transcend it."

I'll wager he did not even understand what I said. Why should he? "Don't look for the meaning, look for the use" is an esoteric dictum in Western philosophy. And yet there was what

I was thinking about it as an answer to the koan even before I used it: the doubts.

Still I do not see how the roshi could have got what I said. He must have known that I had no answer from my bearing; or on the basis of past experience. No one gets the answer at the first try. However, I am in a sense "on the other shore," for I understand no-mind and emptiness, and can go logically from one to the other even if I do not practice them.

The comparison between koan practice and painting works with any art—writing creatively, for example. Or living. The koan here is the world or the environment. The amazing thing about koan practice is that it is a deliberate method. Would it work as well outside the environment of a Buddhist temple?

A dog is a dog. It is only a notion that he has Buddha-nature. Thus "mu" is a correct answer. The monk was involved in *thinking* that the dog had a Buddha-nature. When the Buddha said that all sentient creatures have Buddha-nature, it was just part of his teaching: a vehicle. Joshu was absolutely right and being quite logical in saying "no." But if I say this to the roshi I am myself only giving a theory. I have to *show* it, to make it real. That is my problem. Given the emptiness doctrine, one can *infer* what I have just said. It is a matter of logic. And yet that's all right, too. The problem is to show it as well as to tell it. If I simply tell it, I am like a painter who describes a picture he is going to paint. There is a big difference between being able to conceive a novel and writing one. Yet "conceive" is good there. A child is first conceived. Then it grows. Understanding emptiness was a conception on my part (in both senses of the term). Now it has to grow, that understanding, until it suffuses all of me.

But see how "logical" Joshu's answer is. It is not nonsense. All the writers I know have left this out about the koan, except Fung Yu-lan in his *History of Chinese Philosophy*.

53

See how "feel" and "see" are being loosened; or rather, their hold on me is being loosened. I feel this about the dog. I see this about the dog. Either applies. Too strict use of terms prevents the acceptance of intuition as a way of knowing. ——Yet Dewey was quite loose in his usage, so that people cannot read him. Even so, after looseness, then strictness; for there is nothing wrong with strictness if you know how to use it.

Well, Joshu's reply is somewhat clearer. And various ways of seeing this—that it is clearer—look similar but are not. And each helps. Yet how to show this clarity remains the nub. And when I find the way it will sound very like the above little clarifications. On the other hand, you cannot put enlightenment into words. It is a state of mind, a state of being. So if this process ever comes to an end, nothing will happen verbally that has not already appeared. Just more words.

"Aha, I'm enlightened!" What good would that do, except to me? And even then it would do no good. If it were serious, it would be enlightenment.

You cannot work on it deliberately. Yet you have to work at it. The koan is like a mirror. It is like the world. It has to be solved, yet it is you who solve it. It has its answer, yet you "find" it. And when you do you will know it. How? Why? How do you know when you've got anything? Smallpox, money, the sum of an addition—

I can feel it growing. The koan? My solution? Must be a little like pregnancy. And do the Japanese not refer to koan exercise as letting the womb grow?

I know damn well what that "mu" means. How can I show it? Show what—my knowledge or the meaning? How do *they* differ? You see, the question "What does that 'mu' mean?" is a philosophic puzzlement. It is like the monk's question. It shows doubt. Yet it does have an answer, as do the doubts of a neurotic. Doubts inactivate us. When we can act again, they

22

23

54

have gone. Well, how about me sitting here with this damn koan? Why don't I get going? Drop it and leave? That is like *telling* a man that he is suffering from unresolved Oedipal conflicts. He will nod and go on suffering. Philosophical questions have to be lived through. You cannot or do not just drop them. So Wittgenstein could not just *say*, "The riddle does not exist." He had to show that it does not. Hence his method as exemplified in the *Investigations*, which was Wittgenstein working, as well as Wittgenstein working on others.

So koans grew naturally and then were turned into a method. If it suffers from a difficulty, it is that this is "unnatural." It is imposed from without. Yet I do not suppose it would work if the zen student were not interested and himself in the grip of some puzzlement.

I now think one might speak of degrees of solution of a koan. That's a strange phrase, but the business is a strange one. What I think one can get, and receive a mild thrill in getting it, is an intellectual solution. You can, so to speak, see the point of the koan, but in a kind of conceptual way. The final solution comes when the answer is no longer just seen but is felt, too; when, so to speak, it is a solution from the whole of you. And that would explain why zazen is so important a part of koan exercise. Satori—enlightenment—are, if this be correct, not mental states. They are mental-physical states.[15] (Another reason for seeing that the claim that Zen Buddhism is an intellectual form of Buddhism is true but highly misleading.) Without the practice all you have is intellectual understanding. That is why so many people can now read Suzuki and nod their heads. Intellectually we are ripe for such an understanding. Fifty years ago the average Western intellectual would have, and did, poohpooh such notions as emptiness, no-mind, and egolessness. Now many do not. They can listen to them and understand them, as though they had learned a new vocabulary. But that is a far cry from Zen Buddhism and the zen experience. These involve more than understanding. They involve a psychological shift to a new *way* of understanding, and that way involves the physical as much as it does the mental. Zen literature is full of the effect of the mind on the body and vice versa, as is that of psychosomatic medicine. But in the West so far the contact with Zen Buddhism and possibly the zen experience has been only intellectual—only mental. We have, so to speak, understood only *about* it, and that is characteristic of our way of thinking. So far, as the roshi said, the Zen boom in the United States is just a firecracker. And it will remain so until something physical sets in which goes along with the theory. Zazen, or something like it, and other nonintellectual things. But how is that going to happen? We do not have time for it; and with us practice and theory, certainly in philosophy, are too far apart. Mind-body dualism. The intellectual problem was solved long ago, by Spinoza. In practice, in philosophy we remain mind-body dualists. Perhaps one might say that, in fact, *we* remain mind-body dualists. *We* do? I do.

Look at all this talk. What about the koan? Don't I just have to settle down and work with it? Nothing outside can help. No books. You cannot turn to anyone. Another reason for the Buddhist claim that all is mind. If you interpret this ontologically you get a fantastic metaphysics (theory) which runs completely counter to the empirical evidence. (Yet mysticism is the limit of empiricism. Carry the latter far enough and you get the former. Also, the mystic is he who really accepts and lives by the evidence of his senses. He is not in the clutches of a theory as is the empiricist.) Interpret the all-is-mind proposition psychologically, however, and it makes sense—in more ways than the one that has just now appeared.

It *is* easy to interfere with something that is going on; to "doctor" an idea, for example. It is awfully hard to let some-

26

56

thing like a koan live, and to let yourself live. To go along with whatever may be going on, to wait, to work at it and yet not to work at it, to be receptive.

Transcend existence and nonexistence (life and death?). What did he mean by that? Get beyond those ideas, yes. But how does one *do* this? Practice. Long practice. You cannot say, "I am beyond" and be beyond. I see now that I am cheating by not doing more zazen. It is not just meditating as one does in the sun. It is doing that physical thing, too (concentrating). How do you get beyond ideas (save in sleep and running, for example) except by something like zazen, the practice of being without ideas? As such it can be done in any position. Sitting and breathing in a certain manner may just help it, or be introductory to it. However, customary ways of sitting help to induce old habits; of thinking, for example.

Hard, hard to get working on the koan. ——You have to show that the question about the meaning of "mu" is both silly and not silly. That is a contradiction, and getting in, through, and around it is the trick. Or accepting it. Joshu's answer is contradictory; that is, it contradicts a statement by the Buddha. Yet it affirms what the Buddha taught. No! And in the "no," yes. It is not only to instruct the monk; it is meant to exhibit or does exhibit, Joshu's Buddhism, enlightenment.

Notice how the one-hand-clapping koan and the pine tree koan differ from the *mu* koan. The one-hand koan is a contradictory or a nonsense question. The pine tree answer seems irrelevant. It does not contradict the question that prompted it. It just does not seem to be any answer to it. But this is going at it logically, isn't it? Seems that all one can do is to sit and concentrate. On what? On the contradiction, trying to get wholly beyond it. You cannot just forget it and be thus beyond, for Joshu did not ignore the monk's question. You have to see through it and accept it. ——Odd how you can see and describe just what is to be done and not do it. Shows how verbal we are. Also shows how hard practice is. But one knows this from swimming, etc.

I cannot see how Joshu could have answered differently. But why could not Matsu have said: "There is a frog in the garden" instead of "There is a pine tree in the garden"? Does "pine tree" have some special use?

See how I tend to treat you, koan, as a puzzle? A riddle? ——Why did I not say to the roshi, when he said, "Transcend existence and nonexistence," "You have just given the meaning of 'mu.'"? How about *that*! If I had said *that*, right at that moment, I would have been enlightened. (To say it, not to become so at that moment; unless that answer just came out.) Oho! Instead of which I sat there puzzled and went away wondering whether he had understood *me*. I did not understand *him*! He throws one at me and I fumble. (I am sure that this is it.) What the koan exercise can do, therefore, is to train you to listen to the other fellow. Hear *just* what *he* says. Don't interpret.[16] Listen to him. Here I talk of listening to the koan and do not listen to the roshi when I am with him. I can imagine that you would get a grand feeling if you did once listen at the time *and* answer immediately, without reflection, without mediation. How simple! Forget the information about the koan having only one answer. Do not treat it as a puzzle.

This fits with the above, that it takes a long time, that all you can do is sit. There is no *problem* to be solved. There is getting ready to listen and to spit out an answer, to show that you recognize he has just given you the straight stuff.

Here we also see the difference between solving a koan and painting a picture. There are resemblances and differences (as always). "Solving" a koan is getting ready to listen. You do not solve anything. And that is why it takes two to play the game, and why one should go to sanzen as often as possible;

and why I have been told to watch the roshi carefully, everything he does. ——So does the artist listen carefully to his subject, noting every aspect of it. In the painting all this comes out for us, who do not paint, to see. I cannot "view" art well because I cannot "listen" well.

You do not solve a koan. You learn to listen. And you know full well that knowing this is not going to help you in sanzen tomorrow. It has got to be, not a part of you, as knowledge is, but *all* of you. *You* have got to listen.

I still do not see the classical answer part of it. But do not worry about that. It will fall into place, too, when you can listen to the whole affair. (Herman Hesse was quite right in *Siddhartha*. But just being *told* to listen will not do it. You have also to listen.)

Once you have learned to listen, you can talk small talk. For the big talk is with yourself. It is reflective. It is philosophy.

So, I would have shown that I know what "mu" means if, when the roshi told me, I had said, "That's it." Now, you cannot plan how to react tomorrow (though you will, and are doing it right now). For then you will react according to plan, you will respond to your plan and not to him (and what he says is him, or a part of him). That is why sitting to empty your mind is important. Empty it of *all* ideas, plans, etc., etc. Only then can you listen; or respond to him, if you want to put it that way.[17] You may now say that you respond with your mind, but if it is a *response* (i.e., automatic) your mind is a no-mind. Ideas become our minds, and ideas cannot "respond" except to other ideas. To respond to people and to things, our minds have to be free of ideas. This, again, is not to say that ideas are bad. They are fine. They are just not everything. Remember how Zorba the Greek could catch sight of a wave. So one can learn to listen by just going out into nature. You only go to school to learn ideas. Nature can teach you to listen if you will let "her."

59

Now, see how things keep unfolding? The day before yesterday you thought you had it when you discovered the question: What does the "mu" mean? But the roshi asked that the first day. You just did not listen. *And* he gave you the answer (you found it all quite mysterious): Go beyond existence or the idea thereof. How? By listening, or being able to. It is not the koan you are working on. It is you. Hence again, zazen and the physical. Hence again, it is you who do it all. "It's all in the mind. Mind is all."

See how I was looking for the meaning in what the roshi said, instead of using it? After all I have said of this dictum, it turns out to be a purely intellectual affair with me. What does he mean? What *does* he mean? Hell, he said it. He *means what he says*. Words do not mean anything but words.

No wonder there is a series of koans. One may be enough to give satori. But to do it, really to listen, takes years of practice. (Really listen? That is to listen all the time. So much for "really.")

How wrong to think that Easterners got onto this because of their *language* (remember Russell in "Logical Atomism" about the influence of the subject-predicate structure of language). You can be wrapped up in yourself regardless of the language you speak. It is being human that does it; that is, just using words does it. Any words. Their shape and the ways in which they are put together (the structure) don't matter. However, it is also the subject-predicate *idea* of the structure of our language that has influenced us, not the structure itself. It is a *theory about* that structure worked to extremes that has done it. How far wrong I was in some things I said in "Zen and the Work of Wittgenstein"![18] America is close to Oriental thought as much because she is a continent as otherwise.

The goal is not solving a koan. It is to learn to listen. But do not get snared in this idea and start responding to *it*.

33

How I was caught up in the logic of the koan! The goal is to learn to listen, to be egoless, no-mind. It is not to *solve* koans. And beware of saying that I now know what the *goal* is. Then you will start working for a goal and never listen. ——You see, all this *has* been said before. The thing is the doing.

Tomorrow I will try to listen in sanzen.

Sitting quietly, the roshi listens.

Prepared to watch him carefully, I say, "You gave me the meaning of 'mu' yesterday."

He smiles and leans forward. "How is your meditation going? How do you feel? What do you think about as you meditate?" Nothing about the koan.

What can I say? I tell him how I feel.

"How about your legs during zazen?"

"They hurt."

"You have to get that 'mu' down in your stomach and concentrate on *it*." He smiles.

It is a fascinating business. I laughed after today's interview until I nearly split. Either the roshi is not taking my work seriously or his listening to me was extraordinary. Further, I did respond directly after all (without interpretation)—although look at the questions. The work is also fascinating because you do not know what the koan is going to reveal next, or what you are going to get out of it or out of yourself.

Now I am puzzled about this. The answer to a koan has come to seem unimportant. In a sense we know the answer. And yet there still must be an answer I do not know for the koan I am working on.

On the other hand, I can well imagine that the first time one responds to the roshi showing enlightenment (i.e., directly) would be a great experience. It is not that we do not respond directly. Children do it all the time. It is rather that one would respond directly knowingly, or knowing it, or consciously. I have realized lately how little we do respond directly as adults. When you respond to a flower, it is usually a response to it as a flower, or as a thing of beauty, etc. And when we do as adults respond directly it is usually as a child does, unconsciously. As soon as we become conscious of what we are doing, or in what we are doing, it becomes difficult if not impossible to respond directly.[19] Small wonder it is said that zen study is interminable.

Today, after the short period of zazen that follows sanzen, I went to the roshi's room to bid him good morning and to smoke a cigarette with him. (Thereafter I usually did this every day.) During our conversation he told me that the motto for zen study in Western terms is "know thyself."[20]

In rather sociological terms the matter looks somewhat as follows. Everything in the process of growing up works to make us not know ourselves, and to build up layers of such ignorance in the form of ideas and habits necessary for survival. It constantly makes us plan and calculate and figure and remember. Thus just by living you keep losing sight of yourself, even if you have for one moment ever become completely aware of yourself. "The unexamined life is not worth living." Some writers, such as Blyth, have been right about this: zen is not limited to the East. It runs through Western literature too. All the East has that is special is a *method* (of meditation) for coming to self-awareness.

Now notice how I have drifted from the koan and hence from myself into a concern with the *idea* that the koan method *is* a process of coming to know your self. My self. Get back to the koan, that is, to myself. Away from the ideas.

I realized this morning that yesterday's work was inadequate, although it felt so good at the time. My understanding would deepen. It was not only that there is an answer and that I do not have it. It was not only that I knew it would take a long time to *be* enlightened as well as to understand it. It was also that I knew I had more to unfold intellectually, so to speak. "To deepen my understanding" is a good phrase for this. And you might say that you go on deepening it until it is all through you. Mind and body have merged in this sense. It is not that they really merge. It is that your understanding becomes you instead of froth on the top of your mind (head). You become an understanding person instead of having understanding.[21]

34 Body and mind merge, too, when the life of the mind becomes spontaneous, as is the life of the body.

That was good, seeing that I did not understand use as opposed to meaning very deeply. Learned that from whom? Koan? The roshi? No, self. Neither of the first two told me.

Sitting quietly, the roshi listens.
"I have nothing to say this morning."
"You have to go beyond existence," he murmurs.
"Yes, that is exactly what the 'mu' in my koan means."
35 "Of course," he repied, "But that is a matter of understanding. You've got to *be* this way. You've got to get beyond existence down there." And he points to my stomach.

36 When these people speak of getting beyond existence and nonexistence, their language is imprecise. As a logician I know this. What they mean is that you have to get beyond the *ideas* of existence and nonexistence—that is, beyond "existence" and "nonexistence." This means that you have to get beyond ideas in general, since the ideas of existence and nonexistence are taken to be the most general, and hence in a way representative, of all ideas. That is to say, you have to get to the intuitive, to feelings, to realities, to the guts of the matter. A tremendous amount of misunderstanding has resulted and consequent non-

63

sense been expressed about Eastern thought because of this lack
of precision. When the Buddha says, for example, that you can
learn to escape the wheel of life and death, the cycle of birth
and rebirth, people have thought he means: to enter Nirvana,
which is a *place* where you are immortal. They have also supposed that his view presupposed reincarnation, and that you
keep coming back to this life until you are saved. I am sure
that this is not meant at all, although Easterners believe *literally*
in reincarnation. What is meant is not something ontological
but something psychological. Escaping the cycle of birth and
death is escaping the cycle of plans and frustrations. It is simply
good psychology, and is why Freud could say of the Buddha
that he was a profound psychologist.

This misunderstanding is also, I feel, one reason why Zen
Buddhists have claimed that the Buddha had an esoteric teaching, one that can be passed on by word of mouth only, or only
from person to person. When it gets in to the books it gets mis-
understood. Then it becomes ontology and metaphysics, whereas
it is simply good psychology. It is teaching, not doctrine. And
that is why it is misleading to say that Zen Buddhism is a
religion.

To get back: it is either spooky or downright fine the way
in which the roshi is always a step ahead of me. I know now
all about making the understanding real, making it a part of
yourself. I know that it just does not suffice to understand the
koan intellectually. That is the trouble with intellectuals: their
ideas are not real for them. The ideas remain just ideas and the
intellectual becomes a miser with them. This is a disease, just
as taking a teaching ontologically instead of psychologically is.
So look where that puts me: very nearly where I started.[22]

What a job looms! And this is where zazen comes in and
makes sense. You keep straining both physically and mentally
until you break through (and then continue to break through)

64

from the purely mental to a blend of the mental and the physical. ——Seen this way, there is nothing new for us about Zen Buddhism but the method.

"Zen" can replace "life" in many contexts, for many of the things you say about zen you can say about life, and often when you are talking about zen you are talking about life.[23]

This morning the roshi joked about my sore legs. He went on to say that a supple body goes with a supple mind. He continued: You should keep up your work when you return home. That is, sit for twenty minutes or a half hour a day. That is enough if it be done regularly. It will relax you and you will sleep better. That gives *you* twenty-three and a half hours a day, and a half hour for your spiritual life. After a while that half hour will spread. Not that you will sit any more, but its effect will come to pervade your ordinary life. ——So the mystery goes out of "spirit."

Aha— You thought you were getting to understand people. But *people*. With *truths* (theories). That is all right and useful. But now you are trying to empty your mind so that it can respond to a particular person. (This is a report, not a theory.) Now you want to get beyond truths. And not to *people*, but to *a* person, a flower, a rock. And to let it "speak" to you.

A new interpretation of "seeing things as they are": it is not as they *really* are independent of us; it is just as they are with a little clear sight—that is, without the ego pushed in. We really need several terms: self, ego, and so forth. You can be egoless; you are always a self. So the word "self" gets loosened. Of course, we do use these different terms, but too often as synonyms and not *as* different terms.

So, too, you can see "things" in philosophy. No reason to suppose that enlightenment helps you to see only people and things better. Why not ideas and theories too?

The matter about the different languages (escaping the wheel of birth and death, learning to avoid pain and frustration) is radical empiricism. There is only *this* life and different ways of dealing with it, or getting at it. And it is infinitely varied, not just one way in which we *think* it is. So my notion that metaphysics is just self-examination is empirical. However, first note that people who think metaphysics is ontological are dualists. They believe in two worlds, the empirical and the super-empirical; in becoming and in being. But you have to be careful here. For being empirical, thinking that there is only one world, is likely to hide its variety and result in dualism again, this time that of myth and reality. That is what the hardheaded philosophers do, in fact if not in theory. So it is not *only* that there are many languages that mean the same. There are also many languages that deal with just the one world, but *mean* different things. And there is a basis for understanding Spinoza's insistence that there is an infinity of attributes. As dualists we can think of only two. Given ultra-empiricism, one must expect more. Spinoza a rationalist, eh?

Again, there is nothing wrong with ideas so long as you do not get caught up in them—the true or the false.

I think a good part of zen study would be to have a single flower in your room. Why a flower? Because it will perish and force you to get another. There is nothing inherently divine about a flower, or beautiful. But other things last longer and you cease to look at them.

Zen people may not have invented this one-flower or simplicity practice. But it fits with zen (life). If you have many things, then you do not look at any one of them. Thus you get separated off from your surroundings. This shows another cause of dualism. It also shows that the Zen Buddhist is not retreating from life, but going back to it. The way leads through the self, that is all. ——This is another interpretation of "mind is all."

38

66

Notice how much more there seems to the *mu* koan now than when I first read it a year ago. I have known for some time about making my understanding real, but have drifted aimlessly. The koan is straightening the craft out, as a rudder does. And after all, is that not all the koan is? Looking for the answer to it is like looking for the meaning of a word! I have in mind that some day I will say some magic word and the whole world will open up. (There may be a word or two, but it is the getting to where you can say them that counts.) This is part of the being obsessed with "ideas" stuff—anything that clutters up the mind. ——I repeat: there may be such a word, but do not let thoughts *about* it influence you. ——So then I think: what *is* the word, what is it?

The discarding of truths = getting rid of values and attachments, too. So in a way it equals giving up your soul, that is, your ego. It does not mean, however, to cease using the truths when they are appropriate. It simply means: do not be attached to them. So the word discard is unfortunate. And it is not that you lose a life to gain a life; you just find that you can use the first without being used by it.

Sitting quietly, the roshi listens.
"The 'mu' is I."
The roshi smiles wryly: "There is an old saying in German philosophy: Was ist das Ich?"

39

I had thought that this answer for the koan had some relation to "I am the word," and hence that I had arrived at it by some logic. But I thought I would try it.

He shoved the business right back on me. Thus does a roshi both help his pupils and not help them, which is another form of the basic contradiction through which one must "see" for the zen experience. You have to get beyond logic. (I cannot help thinking here of Wittgenstein—"the civil status of a contradiction"—and Heidegger—we may have to go beyond logic—however much their sayings seem to be related to something different from what I am doing.)

It is remarkable what does come out of the koan exercise. Four or five days ago I sudenly thought: Oh boy, these notes will make a fine book! Look at all the great stuff that is coming out of *me*. Real, human truths. Impressive. Yesterday I saw quite clearly that of course they were fine truths, but they were not mine. I had not thought them up. They were already there in my mind. Deeply implanted. They had been put there by years of reading and listening to others. They are and have been for a long time in the public domain; I was not creating them —I was merely having them come to light. And this is all right, for then maybe they can be used better. In a way, it is to understand them.

This helps to see what is meant by "coming to your pure mind." Get the truths, the ideas out, and what is left? In a sense, the receptacle. But only in a sense, for to speak of a receptacle is also misleading—though I can see better now why some philosophers have done so.[24] This in turn shows what one is doing when one is trying to understand an idea, make it real. One is trying to get rid of ideas. Better: to get to the realities. In a sense you never understand an idea, any more than you understand a hammer. You cannot make it any more real than it already is. What you can come to do is to *use* it. Instead of having it clutter-up the mind, let it become the tool it is. That is why the Zen master can say: The enlightened life is your everyday life. Not yours and mine. But the life you lead when you are untroubled by ideas. When the doubts (What *is* the meaning of it all?) have ceased. That is not to say that the "untroubled" farmer is enlightened. He resembles the beast he drives more than he does the sage. But Kant seems to have been right. To be a philosopher (not just to study philosophy), you have first to ask metaphysical questions, have doubts. And then learn to settle them and be done with them.

My feeling now is that, if there be an answer to the koan, I am a long way from it.

Why did I not reply immediately to the roshi when he said: "Was ist das Ich?"? Instead I sat like a bump on a log wondering, "Yes, what *is* the I?" Now, one may say that I was responding by thinking. After all, he asked a question. But I did not *respond*. I *thought*. Where in that behavior is no-mind? I did not take his words as a tool, or treat them *as words*. I thought and looked for the meaning.

I see more clearly that I am doing an impossible thing: trying to find an answer which is not an answer.

Why am I so smug and happy in all this, being faced with an impossibility? (There is only logical necessity! ——But I am coming to feel a distrust of these echoes of Wittgenstein and others.) Is it because, although I can feel that all the ceremony connected with Zen Buddhism is nonsense, I cannot help feeling that what I am doing is not nonsense? It is real and solid, if slow. And it fits with the past few years' work.

I am trying to break through into not-speaking. Yet I keep speaking! Well, not-speaking is what you are trying to get to, —not not speaking. Joshu replies, yet it is a not-speaking reply. It both answers the question and does not.

It is the difference between "I see" and "I see that . . . ," between direct and indirect knowledge, direct and indirect speech. Good. But where does that get you?

How I wander— It is hard to bear down on the koan. —— Yet I have just as much chance of getting the answer as anybody does.

I still feel now that, regardless of how I do it, if I can respond directly to the roshi I will have something. But is that not being trapped by an idea of what you ought to do? You say that you feel this. Is it not rather that you think it?

Joshu's answer shows what he knows. The truth? No, reality. Scientists know the truth (truths). So I must know reality (myself) before I can answer the roshi.

A note before bed that night The work on the koan seems to have reached a new phase. I keep at it, but little comes out. And I now seem stuck with the impression that something else, I do not know what, is needed. That is, I cannot just go on analyzing the koan and myself. I seem to have reached the limit of what can be done with words, so to speak. I understand the koan well, but I seem now to have to make some sort of a break through the words. I know that to give the "answer" I have to go in to the roshi with a blank mind. And I cannot get it blank as I have been proceeding. I seem, in other words, to be up against a stone wall. Every path I now take leads back to the same point. So I tried just breathing exercise during zazen, just blank concentrating. Nothing to say came out of this.

42

NOTES

1. As explained in the Preface, it is essential to read the Appendix before starting Chapter Two. Numbers in the margins will be referred to later and have no significance here.

2. I put "thoughts" in quotation marks in the text because I am referring to all sorts of things that can go on in one's mind: for example, imagery, planning, remembering, theorizing, awareness of particular sensations. Most people who begin to work on a koan have some knowledge of what might be called the philosophy and practice of Buddhism, particularly of Zen Buddhism. In many cases this knowledge is great, that is, the student has read enormous amounts

of Buddhist literature. In my case I had read possibly a quarter of the Buddhist literature in English, and I suppose 90 per cent of what has been written in English, French, and German about Zen Buddhism.

3. What is the difference between Wittgenstein's thinking out loud and this sort of thing? One feels there was something objective which he was thinking through (the nature of language). But was he not at work on himself, on the picture that held him captive?

4. I have noted in the Appendix the custom among Rinzai Zen Buddhists by which the results of work on a koan are not made public, but are regarded as a private matter between the roshi and the pupil. One can think of many reasons for this, one of which is that future workers on that koan will be misled by any such reporting. I may be wrong, but I believe from my own experience that this danger, though it exists, is small compared to all the influences in a man's life that keep him from solving a koan.

5. One is reminded of Wittgenstein here. The rules for the use of a word may be important in learning to use the word, but *using* a word is different from *learning* to use it.

6. "Philosophical Reflections," *Chicago Review* (Summer, 1959).

7. A fundamental Buddhist concept. The intuition came in a reading of the *Lankavatara Sutra,* when I saw that the concepts of emptiness, no-mind, nonduality, egolessness, and all-is-mind are logically related; when, too, I could read about these things without the feeling that it was all nonsense.

8. The fact is worth thinking over that one can deal with philosophic issues in many different sorts of terms. It may strike a Western reader as strange that we should be talking about Buddha-nature and the cardinal principle of Buddhism in a philosophic essay. It is not strange. It only seems strange.

9. Western philosophical questions may be regarded as koans (e.g., Does God exist?). When they are, you can see why positivists have concluded that they are meaningless.

10. A question Zen Buddhists have asked is: What was your original face?

11. It is well to remember that I am merely reporting here, not stating facts about Zen Buddhism or the technique of Zen Buddhism.

12. For the sake of clarity and at the risk of repetition, it should be said that the word "koan" obviously has two uses: (*a*) referring to an anecdote (such as that about the monk and Joshu), and (*b*) referring to a question about the anecdote (in this case, "What did Joshu's 'Mu' mean?").

13. Compare with being enslaved by a prejudice.

14. In each sanzen interview the pupil recites his koan before giving his answer to it. Hereafter I omit the recitation. The interview reported here occurred two days after I was given the koan. Thereafter, with a few exceptions, interviews occurred daily.

15. As I am using the term "physical" it refers to everything nonintellectual. Hence it might be better to say here that satori, etc., are states of the whole organism or of the whole being. By "mental states" in this connection I mean what we *think of* as mental states, what Wittgenstein called the "gaseous media," which in his inquiry turned out to be the verbal in some of its occurrences (the instrumental).

16. "Listening" is in a way automatic response. Interpreting, unless it be for purposes of pointing to something, is like thinking (in Wittgenstein's way of getting at it) that thought is something unique lying behind speech. It is like believing in the mental as something completely distinct from the physical. Interpreting, when it is not seen as a way of pointing to something, when it is taken as giving the meaning of something, is one way a person thinks who is in the grip of the idealist frame of mind. See n. 17.

17. Think of Wittgenstein's yellow flower (see p. 33). We tend to think a person has a mental image of yellow with which he can compare things till he finds the yellow one. But then how does one understand the order, "Imagine a yellow patch?" The response

comes *automatically*. It is like the business of conditioned reflex. (You think I am a behaviorist, said Wittgenstein.) There is nothing mental going on when understanding is going on. Something mental occurs only when we are learning to understand. The process of learning to understand has misled us about understanding; the process of learning a language has misled us about using a language. Think also of Dewey's "Thought begins when ongoing activity is interrupted." But Wittgenstein seems not to have been trying to set us straight about thinking (understanding). He seems rather to have been trying to free us from misconceptions about thinking, at the root of which lies the misconception about the relation of language to fact. The Zen Buddhist, on the other hand, tries to free himself from conceptions *and* misconceptions.

18. *Chicago Review* (Summer, 1959).

19. The following may clarify what I am getting at here. In the interview reported on p. 61 I responded directly to the roshi's questions, but I was not conscious as I did so. I was, so to speak, lost in the answers. Had I been responding knowingly, as I am using that phrase, my consciousness would not have receded with the answers.

The following anecdote may also help. Once I went to a friend's house, and because it was sunny stepped out into the garden and sat on a rock. It was a delicious experience, but in a few moments I was informed that I should not sit out there. The garden was designed to be viewed from the room (thus I could not see its beauty from where I was), and I was cluttering it up. I stepped back into the room and looked for the beauty of the garden, but now I could not find it.

20. He first asked about my legs, which hurt a good deal during zazen, and showed me some exercises for relaxing the muscles. Then, after introducing the matter of self-knowledge, he talked about the importance of self-knowledge in the relations of people with each other and how impossible democracy is without it.

The impression is growing stronger that the closer one gets to Zen Buddhism and Zen Buddhists and the further from books about them, the less one hears such terms as satori and enlightenment and the more matter-of-fact the whole thing becomes.

21. James: Does consciousness exist? No, or let us rather speak of conscious behavior.

22. Wittgenstein: Philosophic problems arise when language goes on a holiday. One way of seeing the task: overcoming dualism. When you can use a term, you do not think of its meaning. The term is its meaning. A thing which makes one overlook this is the fact that, ordinarily, for some purposes, it is important to distinguish the word from the thing.

23. This suggests, too, that a better way of speaking of the dualism between the mental and the physical is "the dualism of the mental and the living." As noted before, I am using the term "physical" in a broader sense than is customary.

24. It is even simpler than this implies offhand. "Receptacle" goes with the spatial word "out." It is part of the logic of the language used here.

CHAPTER THREE

SITTING QUIETLY, THE ROSHI LISTENS.

I sit and look at him. Finally: "I have nothing to say."

He smiles. "You must be diligent. *A* to *b* to *c* is logic. You've got to cut through that. Sometimes the cutting is called intuition. Just cut. Be diligent."

So I have to break through the chain of words, and keeping notes is not helping this. Yet what I am at is not the giving up of words completely. Joshu said no. It is getting free of them. And I do now feel that I am caught on a verbal merry-go-round with the koan. Curious feeling, as though I might break out and cannot.

I can see how, psychologically speaking, one might be brought to a pitch of tension at this impasse and then break through it by being hit (stories of Zen students being hit). Is this why the roshi said in conversation yesterday that I should have a sesshin?[1] Does he know that now I need something brutal, sheerly physical, exhausting? To exhaust the words right out of me? So I will have to submit to the indignity and the pain? ——Ah, how we protect ourselves!

Yet I am seeing that Zen is not just getting beyond words. It is going beyond *ego,* beyond yourself. So it is more physical than one might imagine.[2]

Yet will it work if I ask for a sesshin? Because then I would be planning, doing it deliberately. That is why sesshins have to be so tough. They have to break your "will." Being tough to be kind.

75

See? I know all the answers. Perhaps it is that I can deduce them from the *idea* of emptiness. But *I* am not empty, egoless. I will not let go of the pleasures, the property, etc.

All right. Throw all your property away. Of course that will not do it, for it is what is *in* you that has to be "thrown away." I could throw away even my clothes and live as a beggar. But that is not it. The job is much harder than that.

See now how I am looking for something deeper? I want to go deeper. Not into the koan. I know why Joshu said "Mu." But into what? Myself? Not exactly. I want something more tangible, more physical. A whole experience. One in which I am completely involved. Does one not get this in sexual intercourse? Yes, sometimes. Then you lose yourself in the other. But I want now, in this koan exercise, something deeper. I can feel now the shallowness of experience *by means of words*. ("Of words"? "by means of words"? Both are right.)

This feeling of want is a new phase. It is connected somehow with having the koan "in your belly." I can feel the going down, down, down, as in the breathing, but I keep getting caught up on little hooks. Thoughts. Why should the *koan* be in your belly? You should, your mind. The hell with the koan. It is just a device. Don't get hung up on it, too. When you get down there the koan will answer itself. It is not a matter of logic.

Down deeper. Every time I start to fall, a hook appears: the thought that now it is coming (satori), I am going to merge with it all. I am going to have enlightenment.

That is part of what really religious people do: they lose themselves in God. It is called having faith. Merely religious people do not have it. Others are concerned with the *idea* of God. It does not matter what you call it, God or reality. Just lose your self. (Making that two words helps, for nothing is going to happen to yourself.) And you can forget the word

43

religion if it spooks you. Talk psychological language if you want.

Something is going on in this. Not just words. But what will I say to the roshi? Forget that too. If you keep trying to find something to say to him you will not lose yourself. When you have done the latter you will say something. Not "you will think of something to say," just "you will say it." (The notion that there is an answer keeps plaguing me.)

So the paradox again: forget the answer to get it. That is also what it means to say that the koan has a life of its own. But don't just see the paradox, *feel* it. Do not worry about the commonness of "feel." There is no mystery here, although I tend to make one all the time.

Having had nothing to say in sanzen is in a way a good sign. If you have something to say it may just be logical, though not necessarily. But just saying something illogical is not enough. *You* have got to be illogical, too. And it is not that people are not illogical either. They are. But they are just emotional then. When they are aware of the world they are usually logical.

But now. See how much of what I am saying here is theory *about* sanzen, etc. The stuff about wanting to go deeper, the awareness (the report) of a feeling, is fine. But the other stuff is mainly dross.

I have a feeling as though something were coming up to meet me. Working with ideas is certainly one thing, and what I am trying to do another. I would not blame anybody if he said, "It ain't philosophy."

I am on a new phase with the koan. I have been treating it as a kind of intellectual puzzle and have been going about solving it in the strict sense of that term. I have been complimenting this by treating it, too, as though it were an object of aesthetic contemplation. Out of this procedure came words and insights which were, I suspect, sights into truths which were already in my mind. By this process I was simply reinforcing or going along with the dualism between subject and object, the overcoming of which is the purpose of the method. Now it seems that I have to do more just plain sitting, perhaps a sesshin, and stop making notes; in a word, get more physical.

Is the koan procedure, therefore, possibly a poor one because it leads to more words? But did it not also lead to the foregoing conclusion?

However, what about that sitting in meditation business? Am I not falling into a vicious circle there too, simply doing what a lot of Zen Buddhists are doing? Another conclusion: act on your own.

Sitting quietly, the roshi listens.

"I know the meaning of the 'mu.' I am now waiting for something else."

The reply: "The answer is up here in your brain. It has got to come from *you*. Concentrate on *mu*. MU.

He looks down, exhales slowly, hissing: "Mu!"

So he knows what I know and I do not have what he has.

I will now work on the koan differently. I am not going to keep notes and sort of think it out. I am going to concentrate on *mu*. I have treated the koan intellectually. I am going to break with that by just sitting.

Incidentally I do not have to worry any longer about having to show *him* the answer (how can I, by what I say, enlighten one who is already enlightened?). Many koans come from mondos, which were often dialogues between two enlightened men. I must *show my* enlightenment, not enlighten him.

45   I think now that merely sitting regularly, emptying the mind,

may be all one needs. ——"I have not thought about the koan for one hour" would be an important statement if true.

Sitting quietly, the roshi listens.
"I have nothing to say."
"You must concentrate the whole universe on *mu*."

In just trying to empty my mind by concentrating on "mu" I have got nowhere.

In a long conservation yesterday with an old Zen student the following was implied: (*a*) koans have a definite answer, and (*b*) I am wrong in thinking that I know the answer to mine (the "mu" means: If you think that the dog has Buddha-nature, you are stuck with words; and it illustrates or expresses Joshu's enlightenment). I thought I had found the "hook" when I separated the story about Joshu from the question about his reply.[3]

The koan reads: A monk asked Joshu, Does the dog have Buddha-nature or not? Joshu replied, "Mu." What does this "mu" really mean?[4] Why is it all translated except the word "mu"? Is that also the sound of a dog barking? Does the "mu" mean Woof? ——But that is treating the koan exactly like a conundrum. It does not jibe with the roshi's "Concentrate the universe on *mu*."

Why is what I am doing now not concentrating the universe on my koan? Because I have not learned to breathe (in zazen) and so be at one with my body? Because I am stretched out at my ease? Yet there is a sense in which I am taking off horizontally from the koan. ——Think of Wisdom's vertical "proofs." Proof in science (reasoning in science), proof in law (reasoning in law), proof in aesthetics ("reasoning" in aesthetic matters). Aha, and "reasoning" with koans: theoretically with your whole being and with the universe, too![5]

You get the feeling now that you would like to be given the answer, as you do at a certain point in working on a puzzle. In the case of a puzzle this may satisfy. But with a koan it will not. Those who have sought the word from those who know have never been satisfied. Knowing about morality is one thing. Hearing that knowledge from someone else when you have not come to it yourself is another. (Only those who have thought these thoughts before— Wittgenstein.)

I feel pretty sure about freeing the mind and letting the koan "speak." Only it will not do any good in this to look at a flower, for it will speak of itself. You have to look at the koan.

Everything now fits except the possibility of a variety of answers to one koan. Yet if it has a life of its own, there can be only one answer. In that Leibnitz was right: each monad is or has within it all it is ever going to become. There are both freedom and necessity. Empiricism and rationalism. Kant brought the two together? And radical empiricism? And Wittgenstein (necessity in logic, freedom elsewhere)? All great philosophic statements resolve a contradiction. They give you both of two contradictories, enable you to entertain both.

Why is not losing myself in what I am doing, as I did when I wrote the preceding paragraph, bringing mind and body together? It is. Why not be logical and verbal? The koan is. Just do not think it needs an answer which is *vocal*. There are all kinds of "words." If you let the koan, a verbal thing, speak, why will it not speak in words? It is in you that the distinction of mind and body must disappear. And it does, when the stuff starts flowing as it was a minute ago. That is letting words have a life of their own. When they do not come, then you are holding them up by being self-conscious.

And the business about *using* words can be misleading. Does one *use* "Ouch!" It is also the case that words have a life of their own. Koan exercise consists in learning to put yourself into

50

51

52

80

the position of letting things (in this case words) have their own life—that is, in the position of being able to listen to them (instead of yourself).

Very well. However, which words are talking now? The koan? Or your old philosophy words? Again, you are not letting the koan talk, although you are letting other words talk.

Now, is the feeling that I will have something to *say* to the roshi, by the means by which I am now proceeding, a bad feeling? On the one hand, you are supposed to show your own enlightenment. On the other hand, you are not to be caught up in words. But if you are enlightened, the koan can speak, and it will speak through you. There is nothing wrong with having the feeling that you are getting ready to say something, except the part of it which has it that it is *you* who are going to say it. You, nothing. The koan speaks; through you, if you will. But it can only speak through you if you are nothing. See? Egolessness. (If you are not nothing, then you "doctor"—interfere with, interpret—what comes out. You try to make it fit something else. So, as a philosopher, you would never be surprised by what you said.)

I am in a condition right now of letting things happen. Ordinarily I fight realities. Do not fight the koan. Get into position to let it talk. This is right. Concentrating is fighting. At least in the way I have been doing it. These monks have said that one should be relaxed when meditating. What about concentrating the universe on *mu*? Well, what is concentrating the universe on it if it is not letting the koan do it all? Remember the doctrine of no-resistance and listening. You can only listen when you are no-thing, when you do not interfere. ——Fine, even if repetitious.

Speak, koan!

But that cannot be done deliberately. I got stuck on the concentration angle. You cannot sit down and say, "Now we *work*." But you can be regular in your habits; do this sort of thing day after day, day after day. Some days you will listen, some you will not. But be regular. That is a way of trying without trying.

"Bring the universe to bear on the koan" = "have no-mind" = "don't interfere." It does not equal "strain like hell." Force, force, force. Not that, but no force. That is letting the universe come to bear.

Letting the words come out, letting them have a life of their own, keeps you from interfering. You could never get all the words out of your mind. It has taken forty years to get them in; it would take forty years to get them out. But if *you* are free of them, if they are living on their own, any number of them can float around in there. You do not have to be *rid* of them. All you have to do is be free of them. (That explains the notion of sudden enlightenment. Gradual enlightenment would be to get rid of all the words.)

A monk asked Joshu whether (or not) the dog has Buddha-nature. Joshu replied, "Mu." What does that "mu" really mean? You cannot just *look* at words. Don't sit and stare. Those are just black marks on white paper. Words are not just that. There has been sense in saying that they have meaning, though it has been misleading too. And you cannot bow your head and concentrate, repeating the words over and over again. Let them come to live with you, in you. That is not mysterious. Think of William James and how you saw, through him, that the ontological argument *is* valid. Think of grief which cannot exist without words. Is grief then just words? No. But neither are words just words (that is, marks on paper, or sounds in the head). Do not ask what else they are. Just let them live with you. That makes sense if you do not stop and look at it. Never ask, what' *does* it mean? Let it talk. Do not bog down on "What does that 'mu' really mean?" Let it, or the whole thing, talk.

Concentrating on it is to bog down on it, to have nothing but the marks there, to keep the words from living. You have both to forget the words and not to forget them. (I am awfully close. That koan is almost being allowed to talk. God, it is maddening!) If you stop with "What does the 'mu' mean?" you are stopped, stuck.

Looking at it as I am today: no mysteries. Just the tough job of letting the koan talk: that is, of being nothing myself, nothing, egoless. Looking at it as I was yesterday was frustrating. Why? Rightly, because *I* was trying.

The answer I have had so far is a theory! *That* is why the roshi said it is all in my head. All the above is a fine theory. Now make it work. I am just as far as ever from passing the koan.

Why should overcoming dualism be so great? After all it is a conceptual dualism. Mind and body are in fact already together (have never been separated). The work is just "psychological." So why anything mysterious?

I have now a slow, quiet, slight, yet unmistakable feeling that something is happening to me. It comes out of the zazen and the life here. I am getting better at something. What? Life?

Sitting quietly, the roshi listens.
"The 'mu' means yes."
"Mu."
"No?" I quaver.

At the time of today's interview I had the impression that "yes" was right. When he handed me that "mu" I should have replied immediately, "Yes." He was following through, and I should have gone a step further. I had the right answer, but when he tested me I funked. Afterward I thought perhaps he was just repeating the advice of two and three days ago to concentrate on *mu*, and was showing me how to do so.[6] But that was later thinking.

If the impression be correct, I see again where "being on your toes all the time" comes in. It is not only that you must listen. It is also that you must be alert, your energies concentrated. You cannot be a receptive blob. You have to be alive, not dead. In a sense the dead listen.

In a way this stuff about listening gives you great power. Anyone who can listen can understand the most profound truths. All he has to do is to be able to listen. This does not seem quite right because it implies that the uttermost simpleton can understand anything. However, it is nonetheless, I think, true. To be receptive is to be powerful. And with my glimpse of this, of egolessness in this way, I feel strong—ready, so to speak, for anything.

Of course, I may have been influenced in my impression by the Zen stories about the old masters testing each other's enlightenment by a rapid verbal exchange in which they behave for all the world like two expert judo wrestlers. But I do not think so. For what may have occurred fits with something else I have heard. You have not only to say the answer to your koan, you have to be able to show it; that is, show that you *know* it is the answer. When you are quite confident of this, it seems, you do not falter.

This gives rise to the notion that getting the answer to a koan is not enough. You have also to build a state of mind by constant practice in which, strangely, you are like a taut string: ready to rise to any occasion. The solution to a koan comes when you can let yourself "listen," be egoless. Then the answer will pop up. However, there is more to it than this. You have also to become alert. The passivity must be strength, too. This is connected with the fact that the life of the Zen Buddhist is not that of a retiring person. And he is critical of many Indian methods which lead to a withdrawal from life and to a life of contemplation. It is also connected with the fact that practicality and hard work are stressed in Zen training.

A function of zazen is to concentrate one's energies. Of course, another function is to purify the mind, to get it clean of ideas. But the point behind that is to make the mind fully able to concentrate on some one thing, without distraction from meandering thoughts. The idea is not to become a mere sloth, sitting on your behind with a vacant mind. It is rather to get into the position of being able to concentrate enormously, so that you can so to speak look with all your energy—so that you do not miss a thing. Usually we miss aspects of things in looking at them, because we do not look hard enough. We are distracted by our thoughts, racing into the future and the past.

A new interpretation of the saying: When I sleep I sleep, when I eat I eat. It is not only being natural, nonverbal. It is also doing things wholeheartedly, concentratedly. So the roshi has given me something again. *Mu*! Concentrate. Not on "mu," but concentrate all your energies.

So the roshi's "mu" was not only to test me. It was also to call my attention to concentration, or did, anyhow. Yesterday I saw the matter about receptiveness but missed concentration.[7] Concentration means concentrate on. It also means con*cen*trate, bring together. Hence, too, the lotus position for meditation.

This practically sets me back again to wanting to do just zazen.

Think how far I am now from where I was several weeks ago when I was seeing through the doctrine of emptiness while reading the *Lankavatara Sutra*. That was fine, but general and abstract compared to what I am doing now. And one can conceive of its getting even more particular and concrete. Until— Wham!—you are right down there at rock bottom.

I can see wanting to lead a clean life in this: a sort of

asceticism, like going into training for football. No drinking because it saps the energy.

Of course if you are egoless the whole force of the universe acts through you. It is not you looking. It is looking. And at this point I feel that training is not necessary, that what is involved is just a psychological trick.

So the "mu" means yes. No means yes. If you *think*, monk, that the dog has Buddha-nature you are lost. The table *is* a table, mountains *are* mountains. Do not just think they are. They are.

What else is there to the koan? Do I have to ask more about Buddha-nature, for example, or know more about it? Is this not just the same as asking: What is the cardinal principle of Buddhism? It is not a matter of knowing more. However, how can words have their own life if you do not understand them? Sitting with a sentence in Japanese from now till doomsday would do me no good. Yet the roshi told me when he gave me the koan that the Buddha had said that dogs have Buddha-nature, so how could Joshu say no? That's the point. How could he? Because the monk was in doubt. Suppose that Joshu had said yes. Would this have quieted the monk's doubt? (I know I have been over all this before, but this is a way of letting the koan speak.) How could it, when the *Lord* Buddha had already said yes, and the monk knew this. So Joshu had to say yes, in such a way as to convince him. So he said no. The thing is delightfully complicated and detailed. The "mu" expresses Joshu's Buddha-nature and answers affirmatively by answering negatively. My "yes" seems to do just the same. (Notice that I have gone along with this study. That is a form of listening. I did not rule it out offhand because it is a lot of nonsense: Buddha-nature, bowing, gongs, etc.)

The beginning of enlightenment is doubt. And the question, What does the "mu" mean? is a sort of doubt. For Joshu its meaning was quite clear. If you can take it for what it is, you do not have to ask what it means. (This suggests that the answer is not "yes.") Yet, although questions which lead to enlightenment (philosophic questions) are doubts, the masters, the enlightened, *answer* them in the strict sense of that term. (I have missed this in the literature about Zen Buddhism: there are answers.) Well, so is "yes" an answer.

Sitting quietly, the roshi listens.
"The meaning of the 'mu' is yes."
"Mu."
Bell.
The roshi adds: "You advance slowly, step by step; but not this way."

I begin to feel the drain of this every morning stuff, rising at four-thirty and going to the roshi's temple. Hard work is beginning to set in. What if you had to do it for years?

Just before I came to Japan I realized that I could live on my own, that I did not have to talk with a Zen *master*. Why then am I struggling so with this affair? Curiosity. A desire to see firsthand, for myself. Dreams of glory about satori. A feeling that this process is a philosopher's stone. The latter two are "bad" reasons. But what of yourself, living on your own, being on your own track? Is this sanzen not pretty much distraction? Not entirely. I have learned, for example, that philosophical questions (as puzzlements) *do* have legitimate answers.[8] I have learned some things about myself. I have come across a new method. Also, however, I have almost fallen under the spell of Zen Buddhism.

(If all this stuff sounds a long way from philosophy, then philosophy is just science.)

There is a good chance that doing zazen has resulted in my

now having to sleep only six hours per day instead of eight. And think of how much theory there was in both the listening and concentrating material I have come across in connection with sanzen. Are there any changes in *me* comparable to the six hours per night. Yes! Mental changes. For example, I feel a certain slight dignity lately. One senses this first, sitting in meditation. What else am I looking for? Something sudden, *bouleversant?* And certainly there is all the loosening up on concepts that has gone on.

Again I see that the *solution* of the koan bulks large in my mind, as though the thing were a mathematical problem. This is being driven by a goal. What of the process itself? So you solve the koan and think you have something. What? The chance to tell a few people that you solved a koan. So what?

Other mornings the roshi's advice has sparked me. This morning it did not seem to. Yet he said step by step, slowly. Is that not what this is?

Of course, I may be misguiding myself with a theory: that the koan has a life of its own. But it feels good and fits with so many other parts of the puzzle.

Why concentrate on *mu?* To empty your mind. Aha, so another meaning of "mu"! Empty your mind. Then you can see the dog's Buddha-nature and not ask whether it has one. This fits with the "mu's" being an expression of Joshu's Buddha-nature. "Mu" means: Forget it! Forget what? Dogs, Buddha-nature, and your concept of it. It is you who count. Forget all.

See how many nice meanings of "mu" I have. Yet not one, despite the way it fits (with my logic) is particularly impressive. However, each one does fit, although this one does not seem as inconsequential as "yes."

Another tack is, how would I answer the question: What is the meaning of "mu"? Do not worry about what a Zen master would say. Yet of course this is exactly what is happening. What does the "mu" mean? Do not ask how I would express my enlightenment (seeing though egolessness), for I have some. But given that, what do *I* think the "mu" means? It means *no*. Its use is to: (a) express Joshu's enlightenment, and (b) answer the question in the only way it can be answered. For, if Joshu had said yes, then the monk would have gone on believing in a theory (and not in himself), and hence would not have seen the only thing that should convince him: the dog's Buddha-nature. So in my language the meaning of "mu" is no, and it has two uses in the context of the koan. (You have to know the background for the koan, that the Buddha had said that [even] dogs have Buddha-nature. Without background, and given "no," the "no" means no—that is, dogs do *not* have Buddha-nature. Simple question and simple answer; therefore no koan and no philosophy.)

Of course, you are being influenced by what you know and believe; for example, the theory of emptiness and the notion that koans resemble philosophic puzzlements. (So that "What does 'mu' mean?" is a question which cannot be given a simple answer, although from what you have seen it has a legitimate one.) So: what does "mu" mean? Then no simple or straightforward answer, but an answer. Forget all else: theories, etc. "You want to *show:* (a) It is an odd question, because in a way its answer cannot be a verbal one (am I not letting the koan speak?). (b) Forget theories, which means— does it not?—forget meanings. (c) Look at the reality![9] (d) Reality!

What does "mu" mean? That (pointing to some object)! And *this* and *this* and *this* (pointing to objects). —But that is not what *mu* means; that is what Joshu means. "Mu" means *mu*. (Problem: how to say a word which is not a word? When is a word not a word? When it is a pointer.)

Do not think of *the* answer. Do not be misled. And do not

⁶¹ *think* of the answer. Give it. Let it come. Say it. Don't think. Act.

The trouble with "The 'mu' means *that*," and pointing is: it does *not*. "Mu" *means mu*.

Now only the koan is in my mind. No thoughts. I am looking right at the koan. Only it is there.—Put it away and what is ⁶² there? Another thought, damn it! No pure mind. Even so I am concentrating only on *mu!*

And for a flash I did! I felt it! We were all one: *mu* and mind and body, I. The trouble is that I can't keep it up. I want to shout "Mu!" to try, but what good would that do?
Mu!

Later Well, I got onto *mu* well. Do not wonder how this is ⁶³ going to help, for that is to *think* again. If no-mind, then no-mind. And with only *mu* there it is nearly no-mind. Do not worry about the answer. That is to think, too. To be distracted. Just *mu* and you, then just *mu*. Only *mu*. Don't think about breathing. Let *mu* become all. Let it, by concentrating on it. Let it by concentrating.

If you are concentrating on *mu* nothing else is going on. That, too, is letting the koan speak. You let it speak by not speaking yourself. And you do that by concentrating on *mu*. Just become mu, no, nothing. (Ah, we are back to theory.)

⁶⁴ Concentrate on *mu*. The roshi said it a week ago, and I am just beginning to. How is that for direct response? Do not worry about the answer. It will come. It is there. You do not have to think it up. Just be *mu* and the answer will come. If you do not become *mu*, "you" will keep the answer out with all your thoughts which latch onto it and distort it.

Now a whole four-hour period with a fraction of a second of accomplishment. Some of the rest is all right, as it drives home the importance of that fraction of a second.

Shall I now answer the roshi thus: "I don't care what that

'mu' means, I am now trying to become *mu*. Should I continue sanzen?"

You do not have to worry whether becoming *mu* will give an answer. For if you do, then you are thinking of "Will it give the answer?" and not of the answer. And how can you think of the answer when you do not have it? All right. Think up the answer. How? Out of nothing? The only way you will get the answer is from the koan. By looking at it? No, you have looked at *it*. "By letting it speak" is the only way of putting it that makes sense to me. Let the words speak for themselves. It is as simple as that. The job is to let them, not to interfere. One way is to become *mu*, as you did for a fraction of a second. Then you are not there to interfere by saying something, as you are right now. When you are *mu* no words will come out. No notes. Because you will have no-mind. It is only when you are thinking that notes come out. I am thinking now, making inferences from "becoming *mu*" and "concentrating on *mu*" and "the doctrine of no-mind."

Why doesn't the koan speak now? Why does "no-mind" speak instead? Because you are no longer interested in "no-mind."

So I am now trying to become *mu*. Despite what I have said before, the answer to "What does the 'mu' mean?" is *mu*. I have seen that answer before and shifted around to others. I am back with it, although I now know it is not enough to say "mu" to the roshi. I have to *be mu* when I say it. To become *mu* I have to concentrate.

It helps a little to add that, when I say "I love you" to a person, it is a fit and proper saying if I am love (we say "in love"). Just saying it is not enough. You have to be it, too. When the word and the thing are one, when the mind and body are one, when there are no divisions or discriminations, that is the zen experience.

Easy to say, infrequent of occurrence. And so, if the answer to my koan is *mu,* and I am sure *now* that it is, it will not do

any good to say it until when I do, the "mu" and I are one. That is, when there isn't Paul saying "mu," but there is *mu.* You can see from this why it would do no good to be given the answer

69 to a koan. You cannot make a man *mu* by saying "mu" to him. (Hence too, in a way, books will not do.)

I shall go in to sanzen tomorrow and say "mu" while endeavoring to recapture that momentary experience of an hour ago.

This morning the roshi and I talked about a Zen monk who has never been successful with his Zen studies, although he writes books and is making a name for himself. He recently suffered a stroke. The roshi finally delivered himself of a little lecture. A plant that bears fruit does not aspire to go higher. Instead it bends gracefully under its load and is not noticed for its high head. Only those who are not bearing fruit ("piling up virtue") aspire to go higher. Then they may have strokes. Lead a simple, quiet life and give your virtue to your pupils. Do not use it yourself. That is to be selfish. And anyway, what need have you of it when you are the sort of man who has born fruit? ——*Virtue* here was used as it is by Spinoza, very much like *strength.*

Sitting quietly the roshi listens.

"The 'mu' means *mu.*"

The roshi stirs, prods me in the stomach with his staff and says: "Go forward, go forward."

It was a feeble "mu," and I was conscious as I said it of my failure to recapture that experience.

70 However, it all seems quite simple now. Sure, "mu" is the answer. And all that I have to do is become *mu.* My word and what I am must be the same. (Note that use of *same.*) It must

be a wholehearted answer. Have I not said that I wanted to realize ideas? This is it for the koan. "Mu" means *mu,* and I have to become *mu;* that is, lose myself in that "mu," be the *mu,* become egoless. The verbal part is easy. I have been trying for something tricky. Just listen to what it says. What does the "mu" mean? It means *mu.* But I have to be the *mu* as well as to say it.

Right after sanzen, sitting in zazen, I almost got that feeling again. I could not get it yesterday afternoon when I went to the zendo alone to try for it after I had had it for a flash in my room.

Now, even if the answer is not "mu," what I have seen is important. In a way to say that "mu" means *mu* is relevant, though perhaps not enough. But do not worry about that. The thing is to *be* your answer. When you and the answer are one, that is being egoless. If I work on that *mu,* get that feeling all come.

the time, then, even if "mu" is not the answer, the answer will

Notice that even the written language tells the same story. The "mu" means *mu.* Not: the "mu" means "mu." That is, I have to *be* the *mu.* (Don't *have* to. Have to, *if* I am to have the answer. Don't have to have the answer. Don't have to have anything.) So my word has to mean something. In this case by my being that thing, *mu.*

How simple. Just listen. The other day I felt that I should only take the roshi a gift when I felt like it, and it should be a gift that I can present to him; not food smuggled in the back door, which is the form my "gifts" have been taking. He does not need food. He does not need anything with all the friends he has around. Still I went out last night and bought a large bottle of pineapple juice. And felt funny again because somehow it went in the back door this morning. As I was meditating after sanzen the head monk interrupted me. He told me that he wanted to talk about my bringing stuff to the roshi. He does not need it. If I want to bring a little gift from time to time, all right. But mainly the roshi wants me to concentrate on the koan. Do not go out and buy food.

My initial reaction was that I was aggrieved. These are fine thanks, etc.! But was I not told in effect what I had told my- self, and had not listened to? Listen to yourself, to your own voice, too. It was a strange demonstration.

Later, when I told another monk about this, he said, "That's right, that is all it is. Just listen. And then see what happens when you do. If you have heard wrong, you will find out." ——How is that for empiricism? Mysticism indeed!

There is a Chinese saying: The gifts in a house do not come in through the gate.

A professor of comparative religion wants to come here to study Zen. What can you tell him? Come here and do zazen. That's all.

Note that the use of "study" there is legitimate, yet it is a different kind of studying from what we tend to do in univer- sities. How do you study Zen? No books. You just sit, work on a koan, and try to be Zen. You do not study *about* it. Yet the same could be true in a university. Our trouble is that we tend to study about things. We do not try to be scientists, poets, etc. Books can help, but we tend to make them the whole of it.

Having to work to become *mu* shows how nonintellectual this business is.

What is the meaning of "mu"? *Mu.* That is all that it can be. Just as "mu" is all that Joshu could have said *and* express himself. Of course he could have gone on about meaningless questions, for example, but how would this have expressed his enlightenment (his egolessness)?

Poking me with the stick today was important. I can some- times feel that "mu" down there; not yet visualize it as I do

72

73

94

one or *two* when I am counting breathing in zazen, but feel it. And that is where it has to come from, from the center of me.

But forget all this. Listen to yourself. "Listening" includes listening to yourself as well as to others and to koans. Listen to yourself. Now you are convinced about *mu*. Learn to listen. It takes energy to listen, and even being able to does not mean that you will listen in every case. But now both you and the koan are saying *mu*. Listen.

You cannot force it into you. It has to come *out* of you. What does the "mu" mean? The "mu" means *mu*. No answer. Yet an answer, and it has many of the characteristics of answers such as Joshu's. I am more than ever convinced that it is *the* answer. Don't concentrate on being *mu*. Just be *mu*.

It's *mu*. It's *mu*. *Mu*. I am not telling myself. It is. *Mu!* And I can see now how enlightenment might be sudden. You have to wait for it, train for it. Yet it can be sudden. After all, mind and body are not separate. But do not leap and caper about. Let the energy concentrate.

Now I see why the eyes are kept open in zazen. Do not shut it up inside. The eyes are the only sense organs which one can close. Why not shut them? It hurts, feels funny. Feels better to have them open. Continuity. Inner and outer disappears. *Mu!* Koan wrote that. I and koan.

I can see the color of that flower as I saw colors with mescaline.

Something has happened! Though would I be writing if it were important? Why not? ——If nothing else I see the flower better, too. Five little stalks and a longer one. ——I am looking at the flower as never before. Thoughts come and go but I seem clear. ——Go along with this. Don't think it is some foolish state. What difference would it make if it were? It is delightful. Look at that flower.

A little too much I in the way? But I have no difficulty in

concentrating on what I look at. Cigarette package, etc. Thought satori was a sudden affair. On and off. Yet why should it not last a long time?

You do not have to shout "Mu!" All you have to do is show that you mean it. You can be quite quiet, or you might shout it. Just so that your knowledge is evident, so that it is out there and not in your head. And it will be evident when every part of you shows it; that is, when it *is* you, when you *are* it. ——I was confused a bit about *being mu*. You cannot be the word, obviously. But you *are* it *in a sense* when you show your knowledge by every part of you.

Any doubts now? A few minutes ago, none. A few flickering about now and getting broken off. What difference does it make if "mu" is not the answer. Look at yourself now. This has been wonderful.

I have the feeling now that all that counts is to show yourself to the roshi. Not quite. It is true: listen to yourself. But if you are asked to answer a question, answer *it*. What does that "mu" mean? *Mu*. Don't worry about the theory of it. Joshu did not. He practiced.

Sitting quietly, the roshi listens.
"What is the meaning of the 'mu'? Mu."
"You have to probe further."

Probe further? Get more into myself? Or is this not the answer? I feel and can appreciate the first, and have little doubt about the second.

But I am discouraged. Zazen is going very poorly. The pain in the legs is terrible. I thought I was getting used to it, but now it's worse than ever. What to do? Lay off? What is the sense in torturing oneself?

Furthermore, I had a good day with the koan yesterday and

75

became sure of my verbal answer. True, I realized that I had to give that answer from "my whole being," not just from the top of my head, and that it is no easy task and might require long training. Still, I felt I had made progress. And now what do I get from the roshi? "Probe further." Yet what elese could he have said. I know that zen study is lengthy.

Further reasons for discouragement. What about samadhi and meditating on pure mind? In the first place, it may be an Eastern cultural phenomenon. In the second place, the interchange between East and West is so new that I am dubious of the translations of terms such as these. Hence, I am finding that we know very little about Zen. And it appears that the more we find, the more we shall see that, except for cultural trappings, it is not new to the West.

However, more importantly, what about the story of Zen Buddhism in the United States? It is quite different from what we call the development of Zen there. The latter is mainly a literary phenomenon, especially strong since World War II, in which something like the "idea" behind Zen Buddhism has become conceptualized. As I see the story of Zen Buddhism in the United States, it concerns a few men with a definite way of life which they tried to import to the States. That way of life includes certain customs and habits, and a kind of training or discipline. It produces men, when the training works, who have considerable insight, who are strong and independent, and who have a custom of meditating which makes them feel good. There is nothing extraordinary about them. They have illnesses, they die, in short, all the things they do one can find in the West, except the performing of their particular ceremonies, eating in their particular way, and so on. They are in possession of no absolute truth, nor anything of extraordinary value. They are just different.

Why is this discouraging? Because I find that I have not yet learned that the grass is not greener on the other side of the road. Also, I have apparently undertaken to build a new way of life (although I did not see it that way before), when I already have one of my own.

Are the roshi's words of this morning sinking in?

And what of my experience yesterday? The more I talk with people who are doing serious Zen study and teaching, the more I find the mystery going out of it all. No mention of satori, and the koan work treated quite matter-of-factly. You are given one koan, you pass it and are given another. I just hypnotized myself into something yesterday. What *happened* was this: suddenly I became sure of my answer. And then I began to see things differently. No doubt about the occurrence. But of course I immediately put an interpretation on it. And that, too, influenced me. Actually I have had the same experience of certainty in working on problems before, although I have never tested to see whether it sharpened my perceptions.

However, this sort of thing is not solving the koan. I keep getting stuck with "listen," and therefore with "look at the facts." How do Zen Buddhists differ from people in the West except in customs, manners, and way of life? They do not. What I am routing out here is the quest for the absolute in me. I *know* there are no absolutes. Yet I look for them in odd ways. The only absolutes are particular things.

Why am I so sure now that "mu" is the answer and that I must be *mu*? (*a*) What else can "mu" mean but *mu*? This assumes that they are asking the question just as we would (although sometimes when the *mu* koan is given the question about meaning does not appear in it). (*b*) I think that I must be *mu* because of the notion of egolessness. Yet if one must be egoless to answer the question, how can anyone without complete enlightenment answer it? There must, therefore, be a stage of egolessness with respect to, say, a given koan. One gets egoless in this respect and can answer this koan. (c) I feel sure of the meaning of Joshu's answer. But that is "mu." Or I feel sure of what the story about Joshu shows: he is trying to knock the monk away from theories and concepts. If he said "yes," I assume this would confirm the monk in a theory (namely, that the dog *has* Buddha-nature). But is not believing all this the result of what I have read? (On the other hand, if I had read nothing, I could not understand the koan at all.) Not exactly, for I can see the point of egolessness from many angles: psychology, metaphysics, logic, and my own experience. Theories are a part of the ego we are trying to be rid of. It is connected, to come at it differently, with no-mind. Now, in one use of "meaning" all this is the meaning of "mu." In another sense *mu* is.

See how logical I go back to being? If this, then that, etc. But if I am right logically (and I seem to be for I can read sutras and understand them), then what is next? Being right bodily. This seems to require zazen.

(I have been over and over this ground. Yet the process does seem to be getting me closer to something. What? Myself?)

I was told today that the breathing in zazen is of extraordinary importance, and what comes out of this rather jibes with what I have been getting at lately. It seems that first you learn your body via zazen. Then you work on breathing. This should be done by inhalation using the diaphragm and a slow exhalation (one roshi says "mu" as he exhales). Control of the breathing gives control of the mind. Learn to handle the body first, then the breathing, then the mind by means of the breathing. The goal is to "bring or drop the mind down into the stomach" by breathing. You finally get so that you can do this at will. Meanwhile the function of the lotus position is to bring the body into a tight ball with no loose ends hanging out. Then, with the mind in the center of the ball, all your energy can be

99

concentrated and brought to bear on whatever you want to focus it on.

There is no way to learn this except by long, long practice.

No wonder I have been told that I would get nothing out of sanzen. It is not only because I will do it for only three months. It is also because I cannot *sit*. (This confirms the impression that I have to become the *mu*.)

Furthermore, this shows how logical my work on the koan has been. Apparently what I have to do is to "drop my mind into my stomach" and then "look" at the koan. Thus, not only can I not give out with that "mu" and be it, because of lack of sitting practice, but I cannot look at the koan properly because of this. I look at it logically. I have to look at it from beyond logic, so to speak, and with enormous concentration (i.e., with body and mind all at once).

NOTES

1. A week of more than usual zazen, and sanzen up to five times a day. See Appendix.

2. See Chap. Two, n. 23. It should be noted that I am not using the word "ego" in the technical sense in which the psychoanalyst uses it. It may also be noted that according to Freud the self is simply known directly and neither needs nor tolerates analysis. This is a feature of psychoanalysis which many reformers of it have attacked most: Fromm, Jung, et al., have insisted that we must not only analyze the ego but also construct a self. Hence their emphasis on "synthesis," "religion," etc. Freud insisted that it was no business of the analyst to provide a self. His sole task was to help the patient cut through the ego to the self and expose it so that it can be as it will.

I am indebted for this point to Professor Herbert Fingarette. I am also indebted to this friend for his reading of this essay and for unnumbered other suggestions which he made, as well as for the encouragement he gave me in this rather peculiar portion of my task.

3. A koan is said to have in it a clue to its answer, called a hook.

4. In Suzuki's version of the koan the question, "What does the 'mu' really mean?" is included. It was not in the version the roshi first gave me.

5. See, for example, John Wisdom, "Gods," reprinted in A.G.N. Flew, ed., *Logic and Language* (New York: Philosophical Library, 1953).

6. See above, p. 78.

7. See above, p. 82.

8. For the way in which I got to see that philosophic questions have answers see above pp. 49, 53, and 54. Having distinguished between the anecdote about the monk and Joshu, and the question about the anecdote (What does the "mu" mean?), I saw that the monk's question about the dog and Buddha-nature is itself a koan or philosophic question. And it has an answer, which is "mu."

9. I *believe* this: reality is what counts. Oho! Reality = value. "Reality" = "value." Those who have said that values are real are right; that is, values are important. The mistake is to think they are all that is important. Why a mistake? Because there are things which are not values. It is just a matter of evidence.

CHAPTER FOUR

Sitting quietly, the roshi listens.
"Woof."
There is quiet for a long time.
"Mu. Go on, go on."

78   This is how it goes. "Mu" as an answer suddenly seemed too logical. Of course "mu" means *mu*. "No" means no. "Woof" is much better. (*a*) It is illogical, (*b*) there is a hook in the koan in the form of "dog,"[1] and (*c*) who thinks about the dog, who considers it, when it is just what should be considered when its Buddha-nature is in question?

One of the monks told me the other day that it is impossible to solve a koan without a roshi's help, because you will be misguided by the line your ordinary thinking takes and it will stick more strongly the longer you pursue it.

79   On any answer vs. a classical answer: true, the first allows for spontaneity; but it leaves out the fact that a koan has a life of its own and that discipline is also important, inner discipline which is connected with the koan having a life of its own.

Do not be misled by the pine tree answer to the cardinal principle of Buddhism question. You may not see its "logic," although you see how it is an expression of Matsu's enlightenment. Hence, it leads you to suppose that any commonplace answer would have done.

"Woof" also looks like a logical answer, although it is a step beyond the "mu" answer.

So what does the koan say? Do not *think* about Buddha-nature. Does it? Are you satisfied with that? Is that not what your theories about Zen indicate, what you learned before you came to the koan? The thing says: Does the dog have Buddha-nature or not? (Background: the Buddha said "Yes.") Joshu replies: No. Why? Because if you think it has, you will not see it. The garden is lovely, but when I am told that it is and how to look at it, I cannot see its beauty. That is the meaning (use) of "mu." Is it not also: "Look at the Buddha-nature"? So "Woof."

And did the roshi not growl his "mu" this morning?

What does the "mu" mean? The whole point is *not* to say what it means *and* at the same time to answer the question; that is, say what it means. I have not seen this clearly before and have tried to say what the "mu" means (hence, *mu*). The second part, which makes up the contradiction, I did not see before I came to the koan. Then I thought: no answer is given to a koan (by means of uttering an irrelevancy or something contradictory) in order to avoid concepts. (That is, the old teachers did not answer the questions put to them.) That is correct. But it is also correct to answer. The kind of thinking which is necessary, therefore, is one that can deal with or see through a contradiction. That is why it is "illogical" thinking. In logic we avoid contradictions. In zen we see through them or *think* them through. This defines the distinction between the two kinds of thinking (indirect or mediated, and direct), for logical thinking (indirect) uses concepts and must therefore avoid contradiction. In direct thinking concepts are not used, for it deals with and does not avoid contradiction.

Getting beyond concepts to reality is not the same as this. I am interested, therefore, in two different though related processes.

However, seeing that there is a contradiction and that one has to go through it is one thing. Doing it is another. But this, too, is why it is said: in Zen one leaves one's senses (reason). Sensible affairs (reasonable) are logical matters. You have to drop this in order to deal with the illogical (contradictory). And it is practical because life, although not the same as the illogical (it is a–logical, beyond words), is like it. The problem of evil, for example. The problem of death (why do the living have to die, how can life and death be part of the same process?).

By God, the problem of evil is a koan. At least, it could be part of koan exercise. Koan exercise = practice in dealing with the contradictory; hence, with life. Koans properly speaking (i.e., the question together with its answer) are records of the solution of a contradiction (note that use of *solution*). The answer to the death koan: that is how things are. You have to accept them. Hence the doctrines of no resistance and no-mind and egolessness. However, it is one thing to see the answer and another to accept it (and therefore *be* it, being it = acceptance). Hence, too, the doctrine of listening. To be able to listen is to be egoless. Strong-willed (ego-filled) people cannot listen. Hence, too, no dualism; that is, the answer must not be only mental, you must accept it (i.e., it must be a part of all of you).

This is all that all this means. See how the parts fit: no dualism, no substances, no-mind, egolessness, listening, accepting, and no resistance. But this does not help you to see through the particular contradiction. And, furthermore, you have seen most of it before.

Here is another reason for there being various koans, and why the solution to them all is both the same and not the same: there are many contradictions. Life-death, good-evil, beginning – no-beginning, etc. Because you have seen through and accepted one is no guarantee that you will see through the others.

Is the *mu* problem a life issue like that of evil? Can five hundred such paradoxes exist? If *mu* is a life problem, it at least sounds like the meaning of life paradox. (It has and it has not meaning. Why? You supply the meaning by talking.) So supply a meaning for "mu." You supply it. All right, but there must be a clue somewhere. I am willing to supply the meaning, thus I am half through the paradox. Which meaning shall I give it? For does it not have some say in the matter? I can give my life meaning, but I have to obey its laws.

So it may be seen in another way how the koan might have just one answer *and* how you have to listen to it. You cannot manipulate it the way you do symbols in a syllogism. You have to accept the paradox and get through it by the "hook" in it.

What do you mean, accept the paradox? In the case of the problem of evil, do you just accept that there is evil? And what is getting through it?

Joshu's paradox was: to say that the dog has Buddha-nature without saying it. He resolved it by saying no. Does that give any clue? And is not approaching it this way like trying to find a formula for resolving paradoxes? Not quite, because you are asking the koan to provide the clue. ——The "problem" now seems quite clear. Think of trying to find a formula for living.

My problem is: to say what the meaning of "mu" is without saying it. Did Joshu know whether the dog has Buddha-nature? Yes. Do I know what "mu" means? Well, that depends on how "means" is used. "Mu" means *mu*. It also means: the dog has Buddha-nature, but do not think that it does. Don't treat the dog via a theory. Therefore (and look at the logic again): look at the dog. Be the dog. Remember nonduality.

Woof. Does that not give the meaning of "mu" without giving it? Well, if you *think* about it it does. But did you not have to think about "mu" to see that it answered yes without saying "yes"? Would not any other word have done? Maybe not, because the written character for "mu" has the sign of the animal in it: four dots at the base. Is that why "mu" is used

and not "no," in translations of the koan? How could it be, since English-speaking people would not know about the character? Anyhow the Japanese for "bowwow" is *wanwan* (written in katakana, that is, not in a Chinese character as is "mu").
——However, research will not solve a contradiction. That is the whole point, in a way. Research is a rational procedure. We need an "irrational" procedure which is also rational. (A person knowledgeable in koans once said that solving a koan is very like solving a scientific problem.)

Haven't you just a theory here: the paradox and the hook in the koan? That makes it a puzzle. Yet what you have heard about them makes them sound like puzzles, even to their being seen to make sense after you have solved them.

The fact that koans do not make sense has been overstressed. We are trying to get beyond sense and hence to non-sense by means of them, but the non-sense is seen to make sense when you get to it. That is, it can be understood. And that is what we are trying to get in philosophy: understanding of life which is non-sense. ——But this is just waltzing about with theories.

The use, or second meaning, of "mu" (to show the dog's Buddha-nature and not to say that it has it) really amounts to yes by saying "no." Thus I have to say "no" by saying something else. Joshu's answer is both yes and no, although its verbal expression is "no." What he has done is to give the thing (yes) another name which is just its opposite, thereby loosening the hold of ideas (words). Thus something else my answer must accomplish is: shake the hold of a word by giving it another use. Note that you do not have to stick with the notion that words have meanings here. What Joshu did was to loosen the hold of a word by changing its use. Thus another clue in the koan: it loosens the hold of a word on us.

These koans are puzzles which are not puzzles. That solves the difficulty about treating it as a puzzle. It is and it is not.

80

So forget that aspect of it. Do not worry about it. And that fits with the overall business: Zen has been defined as doing your damnedest without giving a damn. Do not worry. Worry is ego-involvement.

Sitting quietly, the roshi listens.
"The meaning of the 'mu' is *bowwow*!"
"No." Decisively. "You are practicing meditation, yes? Practice it more and grow up."

Ha, ha! Prrrofound, that!
Grow up. Of course, that is what we are all trying to do. That is the heart of the matter. Grow up, be spiritually as well as physically mature. How, is another question. But *that* one should grow up is to the point.

However, there is another way in which the roshi's remark may be taken. It is quite obvious. When a man comes in to you one morning and says "Woof!" and comes in the next morning and says "Bowwow!"—what else besides "Grow up" would you say to him?

By now I know that barking will not do. I should say that I think it will not do.

How can I say "mu" and not say it? Oh *God*, what is the next step?

There is a third possibility in connection with the advice to grow up. If the answer to the koan is "bowwow," the "grow up" could mean: "*Be* the dog, be a big dog. Your weak 'bowwow' shows that you are not convinced." So I should shout BOW-WOW!

What *is* the next step?

Sitting quietly, the roshi listens.
There is a long pause. It all seems so silly and futile.

"I had something to say, but I cannot say it."
"Mu. You must get the whole universe behind you."

This blockage resulted in a feeling that I wanted to talk at length with the roshi. Man to man stuff about philosophy and life and what not. As soon as I thought of this, however, I realized that it would do no good. What, after all, was there to talk about? Short of giving me the answer to the koan, what could he tell me that I do not already know about it?

Nevertheless, after sanzen I went to the roshi and told him that I wanted to talk with him. I still felt that I wanted to communicate with him.

I asked him whether I could talk with him about what I was doing. He said, "No. We do not talk about sanzen. You may describe the process when you return to the States, but you cannot talk about the actual doings. ——I can see your trouble in your eyes, you do not have to tell me that you are troubled. But you have to do this on your own. It is a spiritual matter. You have to come to an attitude, deep down inside. To talk about it lessens the chance that you will achieve it. You have to overcome what you feel now by yourself. Make an effort of will. Furthermore, I will not descend to talk to you. You must ascend to talk to me. It is the process that counts. People always get eager and rush ahead for the answer to the koan. But it is the spiritual process that counts. You cannot rush that. This is not something new which you are experiencing today."

Then he talked about sitting in meditation. He showed me some exercises which loosen the muscles and make sitting easier. He spoke of the need for being flexible and pliable. Iron, for example, goes through stages of curing. After the first few it is brittle and will break when bent. Finally it gets strong and elastic. It can be bent and spring back into shape. That has to be the condition of your body. And only then will you have a mind like that.

This gives me a fresh appreciation of Zen Buddhism as well as some perspective. Working on a koan might be likened to working on living. Sheer ingenuity will not do it. Many other factors are involved. Further, the foregoing gives a fresh slant on the so-called Zen person. He is simply one who knows how to live. And the Zen experience is the delight which one can get in the awareness that one is living and able to accept the paradoxes. There is no mystery about it, no great mystical experience. One thinks of Zen and the Orient as of something extraordinary and out of this world. Whereas Zen Buddhism was developed by the Chinese, the most practical of people.

So now we have another facet of this business. The actual answer to the koan is quite unimportant. What counts is the process of getting it. And in that process, in a sense, a man is made. He does the work himself, with pointers and goadings from the outside. But it is a process involving the whole individual. And this makes me see how much on the top of our minds what we call doing philosophy is. How really intellectual it is, how much just sheer brain work. And how little, therefore, having to do with the life of a man.

I can feel the tightening up more and more as a result of what is going on lately, this making the affair one of the whole man. The lotus position and the solid feeling make more sense.

Still, there are methods, not a method. This one I am sure can make a taut, strong, resilient being with great perception. There are other ways of doing it. One thing is clear: however it is done, it takes work, wholeheartedness, involves all of you.

Yes, what we have in the koan method is a model for life. The paradoxes, the struggle, the trying to get the answers beforehand, their not doing you any good if you do, the process being what counts. Compare the method with life and you see a lot about both.

Is the *mu* koan a serious one, by the way? Does it deal, that is, with a major problem such as that of evil or of death? It seems to deal with the meaning problem. (No, life has no meaning. Yes, it has the meaning you give it.) (No, words have no meaning. Yes, they have uses.)

With all this, however, I have the impression that I am now at an impasse. I have done all the intelectual work on the koan. I have, so to speak, got beyond concepts with it. Now I am waiting for something to happen, something to flash through. I have been close to this before, as when I said I needed more zazen.

Sometimes now I have the feeling that I am below my mind, looking up at it. It appears as a whirling, buzzing confusion of ideas. I can see the confused things and see how they are ensnaring me.

Sitting quietly, the roshi listens.

I repeat the koan and then sit silent. I know that this is no answer, but I have nothing to say. Slowly he raises his eyes and we look at each other. Finally:

"Mu. You must jump across. Transcend."

Sitting myself immediately thereafter, I thought "nothing." Then "mu" means *nothing*.

With this came a feeling of extraordinary exaltation. Not that I had the answer, but I saw how hard I had been trying to get a logical answer and trying logically to get one. (The exaltation also came from a feeling that I had made a step forward.) I could see that all my answers have been logical. At least they have been logical in the *way* in which I have given them. I am not saying that one of them might not be it, but I did see that none of them will do as I have done them.

"Mu" means nothing. "What does the 'mu' mean?" *is* a nonsense question, and I have been taking it seriously. Thus I got out for a bit and saw how rational I have been and am, and how there is another side. I felt good and light, and it must have shown in my eyes. It is, by God, as though something that might be called a mind is getting free of all conscious accretions (ideas, concepts, images, etc). It was as though I had followed the roshi's "transcend" directly.

In this light it seems quite evident that what is needed to "solve" the koan is meditation, zazen. And how curious that makes philosophy apear: (*a*) there is the old history of ideas stuff and logic; (*b*) there is Wittgenstein's stuff, which seems fairly mental now; and (*c*) there is zazen. *Doing* philosophy seems to be just living. But philosophy as a rational subject in some sense remains, though it does seem terribly abstract and rather silly from where I am now. This also suggests that the solution to philosophic problems is somehow intuitive and not rational. Yet zazen and sanzen are formal procedures.

Odd, the feeling of having a mind and of getting below or outside of ideas.

Also the suggestion of building up force, energy, now makes sense. The energy is needed to make the jump (across to no-mind). It is one thing to think of no-mind and another to have it. Thus again, I should be doing more zazen.

Here too one feels how much zen practice has to do just with one's own life. It is to form an attitude, a condition; that is all.

Seeing that really there is no answer to the koan helped. I have been looking for the answer. Of course, there is and there is not, but I have been on the other side of the coin. ——Seeing that really there is no answer helps, and the "you have got to transcend" helps. What I need is a *condition*. Then the answer will come. It is almost as though you work for the condition (to get the answer) and not for the answer. It is like the hedonic paradox: you do not get ehappiness by seeking it. It comes with some activity. This fits with the notion of the importance of the process (as against the result). It also fits with having no goals. It is not that there are no goals. It is that, in a sense, one does not get them by working for them. This is what we do: we strive and never accept the present.

It all keeps coming back to the same thing. Live in the present. Doing your damnedest without giving a damn is living in the present. This is another glimpse of enlightenment. It is not same superconscious state. It is the ability to live in the here and now (that is, without plans or *arrières pensées*). Sleep is accepting the present without being conscious of it. Enlightenment is conscious sleep. This gives rise to the feeling that what is needed now is *work*. Concentration. Intense concentration.[2]

Nevertheless, a step has been taken. All I have to do is recall that feeling for *nothing* and I know I am on the other side of something.

The step has enabled me to accept today. I am not just waiting for the time to go out to dinner. And I can be, and have been, looking at each stone and flower in the garden. I have, that is, with my meditation slipped into the present. *Now,* do not think of the answer to the koan now. Do not start working again (i.e., reaching out—and *reaching out* shows how it can be said that the answer is within. After all *out* and *in* are in a logical game. And if we start with *out* we naturally go to *in*—to the part of the talk of the truth being within.).

Everything that everyone says is right, provided that it is sincerely said; that is, provided we do not tamper with it (project ourselves on it, if you want). Things only seem contradictory because we assume that a statement cannot be both true and false at the same time. However, it can be, because language is logical but the world is not. The world is multifarious, and therefore appears to us as paradoxical.

To sit here and work on being in the present by, say, looking at a rock is like accomplishing the same attitude by working on

87

112

a koan. Any object will do. However, a koan has the merit of being verbal and illogical (a-verbal) at the same time. Why, therefore, do I not just concentrate on the koan? Not as interesting as a rock? Well, nor is a rock you have looked at for two weeks interesting. Is that why flowers are good: they perish? The paradox again: doing without doing. Surely then, just *any* sitting would do.

But notice, when you just sit, how easy it is to become busy with thoughts: plans, memories, etc. To become involved with the subjective. You do not keep looking out there, at a rock, for example. Yet how about watching a sport? Then you are involved, too. How about a sunset or a fountain? Different. However, you are as busy just sitting as you are in meditation (formal zazen). The koan is a device to get the mind empty except for the koan.

I seem better able to concentrate on a single object lately. Indeed, I have never done it with an awareness that it could be done.

A reason for thinking that just work is needed is that when I try to concentrate on "mu" I so easily fail. I say to myself, "Oh, well, I'll do it tomorrow." So it is not just work. It is also practice, routine. One must get into a habit. But I am at least feeling for myself that there is a "pure mind" and seeing how busy we keep it or let it be. No repose. No wonder it requires sleep. I can just feel the thoughts pulling always at me, distracting me. (That is a good description, metaphorical or no.) One can thus imagine what the mind (what *one*) could do if undistracted, working as we say with full concentration. So it is not only overcoming dualism. It is also being able to be undistracted. And it may be that Westerners are good at this with ideas and Easterners have learned to do it with objects, including oneself. Or with nothing. This puts a different light on the condition to be achieved. Think of Russell's story of Whitehead's extraordinary powers of concentration on a mathematical problem.

In the course of this I am getting to know myself, my distractions, for example. This makes it all sound quite prosaic.

Why does the roshi keep saying "mu" in sanzen? Is he just saying: "No, that is not the answer?" Or is he giving a hint? But that is too dramatic. Yet, if one really listens. . . .

Yes, a step has been made today: the seeing of *nothing*. It brought me into the immediate present for a while.

Sitting quietly, the roshi listens.

I repeat the koan and then:

"Roshi, you have been pulling my leg for three weeks."

A long pause, a feeling that I am being sized up. Finally, a slight shake of his head, and:

"Not yet."

Yesterday and this morning I have made much progress. I have been confident before, but not in the way I am now, that a clear and definite step has been taken. It was really taken yesterday morning just after sanzen and while doing zazen, and the rest of the day went into recovering my balance after it. If you compare what I said to the roshi this morning and what he replied with what I have said in the past and his replies, you will see the step.

First of all, I went in to sanzen feeling different this morning. I felt confident, rather as though I were on the other side of something. Beforehand I was almost caught up again in the trap of looking for an answer, but I recalled yesterday's *nothing*. The recollection helped. A way of talking to the roshi occurred to me and I went in with confidence.

The explanation of the step taken is clear, though it is remarkable after all I have said for years about meaningless questions. (On the other hand, if the step is as decisive as I think it is, it is because I have been working on the *mu* koan for a long time without knowing it.) Here is a description of the step. What I suddenly saw yesterday, or better what I *felt* and saw, was that the question "What does the 'mu' mean?" *is* a meaningless question. How can I say this when I have "known" it all along? Simply because I *have* just *known* it; academically, theoretically, so to speak. Go a bit further. What I saw was not so much that it *is* a meaningless question; I saw the *meaninglessness*. And that, of course, is what "mu" means: no, nothing, nought, void, emptiness.

So I now know *directly* what the "mu" means. I experienced it, am experiencing it right now. The thing has ceased to be merely verbal or a verbal experience and has become nonverbal experience. This can be made clearer by going on to say that in a sense it does not make any difference what I say next to the roshi. What matters is how I behave. That is, what matters is I, when I am before him. I am, that is to say, no longer concerned with words (with the koan) but with a nonverbal thing: myself. If I can go into sanzen with complete self-assurance, be all there (we sometimes say of a person, "He is not all there, you know") and *show* him by the way I am that it is a meaningless question, the koan is solved no matter what I say.

Put the matter slightly differently. I have been working on the *answer* to the koan. I have been looking for that. I have, that is, been looking for more words, or a word. But that is exactly what one is trying to transcend. Now I am not looking for the answer (since I know that there is none—watch for the paradox). I am instead concerned with making my awareness so much a part of me that it is no longer my awareness—that I *am* awareness. (Sounds odd, but it is logical.) And that is a matter of training. That is where Zen training comes in. When that state of *complete* confidence is reached, and when it shows, then the verbal answer to the koan will come. For the koan has an answer.

"To be able to live in the present" is further explicated by "to have complete confidence."

(My projects in coming to Japan have dovetailed. Study Zen Buddhism, do philosophy, and see and do something aesthetic. It all fits, every detail of health measures and so on, with what I am doing now. The new feeling of strength I have noted has grown and I am more aware of it. Thus the koan work is a continuation of something and not something new. The trip is a success. I am not doing things in different compartments. I am doing one big thing.

I have sometimes wondered that my "work" should be in such different compartments: teaching, living, the papers I write. But in so far as the latter was separate it should have been, for it was verbal, not real.

It is a wonderful feeling to have one's life and one's work become one, to see that one works either not at all or twenty-fours a day.)

Now I ask myself: is this that I am doing zen? And the answer is quite simple. It does not make a bit of difference whether it is or not. Call it what you will, it is the thing that is important.

Let us go back to this morning's sanzen and come out again. The roshi paused before saying "Not yet." This is interesting, for I felt as he paused that I had acted properly, and yet there wasn't conviction in what I said. There was a shade of doubt, and the hope crossed my mind that the pause might mean that I was right. I was right in a way. I had not given a logical answer. I had learned from yesterday. Yet even I knew that I was wavering ever so slightly. So he said, not yet.

I have also been misled by the "hook" business. It may be that "mu" is the hook, but what has to be shown is emptiness, naught (and of course that is what "mu" means, not just No). This suggests that any answer which indicates the meaninglessness of the question will do. What is important is to be convincing; hence, convinced.

Another example of how words mislead: you have to *be* the answer. I have taken that literally and have tried, therefore, to be what I am not. To be the answer means: do not lack conviction.

One would think, after all my harping on meaningless questions and "no riddle existing," that I would not have fallen for: What is the meaning of "mu"? But I did. All I have to do now is really believe that the riddle does not exist. In a word, I have to believe in myself.

It does make sense to speak of a leap across. I did yesterday, although I am only feeling the full effect now. I leapt from looking for the meaning to myself, from concentrating on a verbal puzzle to concentrating on myself. I have thought that you work on the koan while meditating. You do not. You work on yourself.

Still I feel myself looking for an answer to the koan even when I have it. It is that there is no answer. "Mu" is the answer. No, not "mu" but emptiness (what "mu" means). And I have to be empty. That is, be full! Come in all there; not wanting anything, not wanting praise, approbation, any thing. Just be there, that is to be empty.

The trouble with "Woof" is that it *is* an answer. There must be no answer. Yet you must say something that shows this. Something that shows you are fully aware of it.

So you are back with "the 'mu' means *mu*." And yet not back with it. Of course it means that. But what is *mu*? Emptiness. If you say, "The 'mu' means *mu*," you will not show emptiness. You are saying something logical. "You have been pulling my leg" is better, although I am not sure that does it. ("If I had a

117

tail I'd wag it"—but that is being "logical" again.) Just say anything that will show you are all there. You—not meaning: not-meaning. Not-meaning is a positive thing. (It is you, it is any thing. So a flower could be shown.)

It helps to say that the meaning of "mu" is not *mu* but the thing-*mu*. What you get otherwise is another word. The use of quotation marks does not help. That it was another word shows up on paper. This is where my step comes in: I moved from *mu* to the thing-*mu*. But how can there be a thing-*mu*, emptiness? (Note how words must be *used*, be transparent. Do not get caught up in the marks on paper, even when they are without quotation marks—or the sound in your head, or the audible sound. No wonder men have found words mysterious: it is their transparency.) Well, emptiness is I without an ego. That is one way of putting it. Another is: realizing that the question about "mu" is a meaningless one.

This brings a calm, quiet feeling. You become calm and quiet. Bicycle slowly, deliberately. What I sense lacking, however, is tautness. It takes energy to be "all there." Otherwise one is calm and detached. There is, therefore, something to concentrating, to building up energy.

Sitting quietly, the roshi listens.
"It is going to be a nice day, Roshi."
"No, that won't do. That is appearance, you understand?"
I reply that I know that, but—
He goes on: "There is phenomenon and nonphenomenon. You have to transcend them. Understand?"

Later in the morning the roshi gave another little lecture. Think about the following.

(*a*) A triangle may be used to symbolize both the meditation posture and what you are striving for in meditation. Consider an

118

isosceles triangle slightly shorter on the base than on the other two sides. From each of the sides a perpendicular is drawn. Their point of intersection gives the "center of gravity" of the triangle. So should your "center of gravity" be low and your "posture" that of the triangle: a figure which cannot be tipped. Contrast this triangle with a similar one stood on its apex.

(b) Your existence is what counts. But you have two parents and they each have two and so on. When you get back thirty generations a lot of people are involved. There is a great inverted triangle with you at the bottom point and all those people piled on top of you. It took a lot of work to produce you. Therefore you are very important. On the other hand, you are dependent on your environment. Everything is interrelated. You are the center of your environment, but you depend on it.

These small lectures give the impression that I have been given a kind of mental imagery to employ in meditation to increase the concentration.

Why did he say that my answer this morning had to do with appearance? (a) Because it was really a wish of mine (that it would be a nice day) and not a statement of fact? (b) Because I was not talking about myself? Whatever the case may be, his remark made me realize how much more of my exterior (hopes and wishes, if you will) I have to slough off or get beneath to be egoless, or to get to my pure mind, as the Buddhists put it.

Later in the day during a conversation the subject of a nice day came up. The roshi said to one of us that some of this person's days were nice and some were not. That is, it is in him, this niceness or no of a day. Maybe when I can enjoy a rainy day as well as a sunny one that will be it. I do fret about the sun, or the lack of it. This is an example of how enjoyment comes mainly from within, or rather the niceness of some days and the ill of others. Days are days, neither nice nor bad. We call them so, and that name is a reflection of us. So the roshi could tell me:

that is appearance. He meant: that is your hope talking, not you. Of course, otherwise it is not an appearance. The hope is a reality too. To say it is an appearance is a way of saying: get to yourself.

That is bending like a reed: taking the days as they come. It is not enjoying the sun or the rain when they are there. Or avoiding them. It is taking the days as they come. And they come anyhow. All the "this is good" or "this is bad" and the fretting are coming out of you. In this way one sees that they are illusions.

94   Seeing this helps to calm me. Think of that triangle. But the wants, etc., are always lurking to trap one.

From this one can see: do not meditate just in the zendo. Meditate all day, that is, work at getting through to reality, under the appearances. Do what might be called informal zazen.

I find it curious that all this seems so real when it sounds either so trite or so like hogwash. Is it philosophy, then, or psychology? In a way it is neither. It is working on yourself to live. You do not do that as long as you are a slave to desires: for example, to solve a koan. It is one thing to read Spinoza on not being a slave to the passions. It is another to cease being a slave to them. All this "hogwash" helps the making of that effort, is instrumental to it. Hence, is it philosophy and not merely a program for it, like the *Ethics?* ——Of course, the *Ethics* may be regarded as Spinoza's expression of his freedom. It sounds like a philosophic theory, and may be taken as such. It may also be his way of saying how it feels to be free.

I see from this how much my former philosophizing had been word games.

95   It now seems that this zen study consists fundamentally in killing off the ego. The condition of no-mind or emptiness seems to be a condition in which one is no longer a slave of the

ego: or, to use Spinoza's language, in which one is no longer a slave to the passions. Or, to expand it a little, in which one is no longer driven by *ideas* of wishes, hopes, fears, etc. Concrete example: how the thought of the expected arrival of a person can lead one to count the days to the arrival date, and in other ways drive oneself silly.

Since my step I have been able to feel distinctly how such thoughts distract, how they make of the mind a booming, buzzing confusion. And I have felt how they are not just mental, how they come up from inside of me. And I have been able, so to speak, to get my mind free of them and to know it directly, which simply means to think without these distracting thoughts, to concentrate on one thing and keep it there before me. I told the roshi: "It is going to be a nice day." He said, that is appearance. I see from this that a day is a day; you find it nice or want it to be nice. Thus he caught me and showed me one of these distracting thoughts and how they come up without your realizing it. And I know now that it had come up in, or out of, my eagerness to solve the koan (as a puzzle) and to be able to say that I had.

From this it is apparent that constant vigilance is required to catch and recognize these distractions. And an interesting result ensues when you do: a feeling of extraordinary calm. The vigilance is "meditation" and it does not have to be practiced only in the meditation hall. Its outcome will be to return you to the world, to get you out from behind these thoughts (that ego) so that you are all there at each instant. No wonder the old Zen teachers have harped on your practical, everyday life.

Sitting quietly, the roshi listens.
"I need no answer."
He looks up, smiling broadly.

"Now go on. ——Mu."

Another smile.

"Remember what I told you yesterday about the center of the triangle?"

"Yes."

Taking his staff, he prods me in the stomach:

"Down there. That's it."

Bell.

Last night I found myself in the act of striving for an answer again; albeit not a direct answer this time, but something like "You have been pulling my leg." So this morning I meditated before sanzen. I meditated on emptiness. I know that sounds odd, but it is a fair description. I was waiting for emptiness, nonego, myself to give me the answer.

Then suddenly I relaxed. I realized that I had been striving again, though subtly. And suddenly I saw that I did not need an answer. I went into sanzen with more confidence than I have before, noticing more details than I have before.

This was another step forward.

The feeling that I do not need an answer jibes with the earlier *theory* about listening to the koan. The more I feel this, the more I will listen. And listening to the koan is "listening" to the thing-*mu,* to emptiness, concentrating on it. That is, it is not so much that the words have a life of their own as it is what they *mean,* or how they work. As tokens they are just marks on paper, say, and have no life.

When you are listening to the thing-*mu,* what are you listening to? Your self. Not your ego, that is mostly words. But yourself. So the answer to the koan comes from *you,* that is, from the koan which is you. When you become the koan, its answer too, then you are through with the lot. Nonduality. *That* is how a koan has a life of its own, so to speak: when you give it life,

97

that is, when you become the koan. If you "become" it, it disappears just as you do (i. e., your ego).

The koan (the words) is disappearing. What is the *koan?* Not the *words.* I have been confusing the word and the thing again (to use that way of talking). "Mu" and emptiness. Of course looking at the words will not bring anything. Look at emptiness, that is, at *you.* (Boy, sounds like nonsense, but it ain't.) You do not have to talk of the meaning of "mu" if you are finicky about that. "Mu" brought you finally to emptiness, or a degree of it. (Repeat: words are quite all right if they are *used,* if they are transparent.) When the koan disappears what disappears? The words. You and the words do not become one. You and the koan (thing, if you will) do.[3] You and *mu* do. That is, you know *mu* directly and not via "mu." And *this* means that you know *you* directly (that is why the Buddhists can speak of pure mind). For when you know you, you do not know *ideas,* although it is possible to know them directly too. I was doing that this morning when out came: "I do not need an answer." It is not that you can forget the koan. It is that you become what the words mean, and when you utter this you are the words.

Now, writing (thinking) like this is not enough, nor the all of it. You need also to sit without writing and concentrate on the thing, on becoming it (empty). Words can also carry you away. ("He was carried away by what he said" is both bad and good.) They leave me in this case, right now, not concentrating on *mu,* which is what I should be doing, although I have been concentrating on "mu."

The foregoing is a seeing through of my own form of the ontological argument. Wittgenstein is right: you have to keep hammering at these things, for they are not just mental. They are habits, and therefore physical, too.

The meaning of "mu" is, of course, *mu:* the thing-*mu.* And

98 that is I. What I am working on now is to show me to the roshi. If I can do it with words, fine; that is, if they show me (not tell him, for that would be my ego talking); that is, if I and what I say are one. That is what to show means: to become what you
99 say. On the other hand, the best way to show a flower is to show it (present it). Well, why not just sit there? That might be all right if you meant it and could show that too. I did sit once; but then only because I had nothing to say, and not because I knew that one need not say anything.

Sitting quietly, the roshi listens.

"What does the 'mu' mean? If I knew the answer I would not be here."

The roshi looks up. I smile knowingly:

"I am here."

The roshi's reply: "That is phenomena again. You have to transcend pnenomena."

100 This process seems to go in cycles. When the foregoing answer, which is like a double limerick, occurred to me, I thought it would show that I had transcended logic.

However, it did not take five minutes to see how right the roshi was and how wrong I had been. I had fallen into the trap of giving an *answer* again. This time it came from my "logical brain." When I said: "It will be a nice day," it came from my affective nature. In both cases, to use this language, it was not I talking. It was my ego. I once thought of the thing Wittgenstein was battling as a many-headed beast (he calls it the picture that holds us captive). You chop off one head and think you are done, then up looms another. So it is with the ego.

101 About the triangle and the ancestors again. The triangle (you sitting) represents a figure which is not top-heavy. When a man thinks too much—when, in a way, his head is too large— he is unstable. The job is to get stable. This fits with the Western

notion that there are insoluble problems, meaningless questions. Thinking too much is trying to answer these. It gets one out of touch with reality. Otherwise thinking is all right.

The talk of the ancestors is simply Western idealism with a twist. You have thousands of ancestors. Therefore you are very important, for a lot of effort went into bringing you about. On the other hand, you will have thousands of descendants. Therefore your responsibility is great. For, further, everything in the world is related to everything else. The actions of others affect you. In turn, your actions affect everyone. The twist on idealism is the emphasis placed by this means on the individual. You are all that counts, in one way. Therefore, it is important to get to know yourself. This is what Zen training is for. The goal is not theoretical knowledge *about* yourself, but direct self-knowledge.

The "theory" about it is so clear and simple. It is only the practice that "realizes" the theory that is hard. To change the metaphor: the device is simple to understand; its use it difficult. The matter may remind one of the difference between speculative-analytic philosophy and *Existenz-Philosophie*.

Well, now, so much for the *theory* about the stuff. What of the stuff? (*a*) By this time the matter of getting rid of the ego seems less important than it did. Maybe it was just a step and one more bit of theorizing I had to dredge up; that is, maybe it too was all part of the ego. (*b*) Also I sense now an aura of phoniness about all this and what I am doing. It feels as though I were trying to wear someone else's coat.

After all, what about my own life? I seem now to be seeking a far-off-sounding place by a far-off route. I have learned about Zen Buddhism. Why stick around?

What else appears important? (*a*) The realization of the meaninglessness of the question about "mu," and (*b*) the notion and the feeling of calm and tranquillity, the getting away from the busy mind. (*a*) leads to: I do not need an answer, although it is connected with (the idea? the feeling?) that there is *quand-même* an answer. (*b*) is easily disturbed. (*c*) Do not look for the answer. Look for what, then? You. How look? What constitutes direct knowledge of the self? How can zazen help? Is seeing my busy thoughts seeing myself? No, it is seeing my ego (yet am I not caught up in a theory with this talk of the ego?).

(*c*) is connected with seeing the meaninglessness of the "mu" question. What I have to do is simply *quit* looking for the answer. However, really to quit is to put the koan out of your mind and stop going to sanzen. Yet there is an answer, something which will reflect or show that the koan no longer worries you. There is the contradiction: you cannot quit sanzen until you have shown that you can quit.

(*d*) I do not have to have an answer.

All right, how can you quit going to sanzen and go once more? That is the problem in another form. And it makes fairly clear the fact that it is useless to seek a verbal answer. Aha! You cannot put the answer to a self-contradictory question into words, because words are logical. Yet you could—if the words were a contradiction, like "round square," or if the answer were not an answer and only became one by showing something.

This makes the impasse, the block, the contradiction more real. I feel it more. It is as though some great effort were required to break through it.

Now, why *do* I keep going to sanzen? For that is all the whole thing amounts to: being able to stop doing philosophy whenever you want to. You cannot stop falling when you want to, for that is not under your control. But stopping sanzen is. It cannot be only that you want the answer, for that is after all only a word or a gesture. No, what you want is to be able to stop going to sanzen (the contradiction in yet another form).

104

126

Now, *this* is coming to know yourself. Why should *you* go to sanzen? I, Paul? Something drives me there. My ego (pride and the false self). *I* do not want to go or need to. *I* like to see the roshi. It is being able to report that I did go and other deeper things that *drag* me there. But *I* do not have to go. I do not have to do anything. My body has to, or does, obey certain "laws" (functions in a certain way). My thinking "obeys" the laws of logic. But *I* do not have to do anything. And that makes sense, although to many people it will not sound so —those who say that I am the sum of my body, etc., etc. I am not. I am I. You want me to specify what the I is. I cannot, except to say that I am I. And I am free *if* I will act. (Hence, the free-will doctrine does make sense, although a lot of nonsense has been written about it by both sides alike.) So, all I have to do is to act.

Now I am knowing *me* directly. A quality *I* have is freedom. (No, do not look for an answer to the koan. Keep on looking at me.) I am free. I need obey no laws. (Therefore, I am responsible for all that I do. Only things that obey laws are not responsible.) (And do not look for the oneness feeling of satori. That is what I have been told to do. Just do what I want. I want to look at me. *And* I have caught a real glimpse: *I* am free.) I am free, that is why no problems exist (but here I get off into theory. Yet, as theory, I can see why they talk of no birth and death and of immortality. I just do not feel that yet); because, since I am free, I obey no laws. Birth and death are governed by laws, are part of the causal world. But I am free, and therefore not subject to law. ——No, no, do not try to make a metaphysic of it, and therefore sense. Let it be nonsense. ——Problems exist only in the phenomenal realm, and of these only the practical problems are solvable.

So there *I* am. Just a glimpse. But keep at it. (Makes me feel heady instead of solid.)

Sitting quietly, the roshi listens.
"I am free." The roshi looks up immediately.
"No. ——*Mu*." Concentrating.

I had nothing to say before sanzen. Bright *answers* popped into my head, but I have finally learned that it is not answers that we want. So I thought that I would just report.

Immediately after sanzen it occurred to me that I should have responded to his "no" by saying "Oh, yes" and rising and walking out. It seemed that I have just *seen* that I am free. I *am* not free. I do not behave freely. I sit there satisfied with his "no,"—I have given an answer, and it is the wrong sort of thing. I did not follow through and was not therefore free at that time. Instead of being able to respond as an individual, I responded as a pupil with his teacher. My ego does this, if you will. This has been trained into me. I react in the stock way. And although I know about not giving an answer, and did not, my behavior did not fit this. My behavior indicated that I *was* giving an answer.

Right now I feel that I should do this tomorrow and follow through on it. This is planning, sure, but it is also being myself. He is right: get the universe behind you. Be strong. Be yourself.

That is a good distinction: seeing your freedom and being free. It makes it clear that being free = acting on your own, doing as you see fit; not responding to the ego, and therefore to the situation, but responding as yourself. I did this some when I said he was pulling my leg. But I did not follow through. That is where concentrate (*mu*) comes in.

About only one or many answers to koans: although there is only one "answer" for all the koans, there are also many. This may be seen as follows. The intellectual counterpart of satori is a tautology (for example, I am I). (Meaningless questions have no answers.) Logically all tautologies are equivalent in meaning. But they *look* different (their *Sinn* is different). So you move from tautology to tautology and then see that they all come to the same thing. Logicians have seen this. What you do in Zen training is to develop, so to speak, the nonintellectual counterpart of it.

Every day put in with writing this down deepens my insight. However, more is needed: practicing it with others as well as alone. In this anybody or anything can help, but especially the true people (the individuals) can help; for they, like a roshi, help to straighten you out. I guess that "bad" people (ones with big egos) can hurt, for they make your ego, not you, respond. A brute thing can help only if you notice it, that is, if you are already helping yourself. However, since it has no ego, it at least does not tend to make your ego respond. Only you can let that happen with a brute thing.

This suggests that we never get rid of the ego. What you can do is to control it, or rather let your self grow. Or just grow.

I can see from the foregoing again that it is not a matter of intellectual power. Anyone can see that certain questions are meaningless, etc. But it takes long practice and great strength to live this way.

Note how relaxing, fighting the ego, and that there are meaningless questions, all fit in with the above. The extension of positivism.

When I think of how weak I was with the roshi this morning I see how far I have to go. There is no hope for an answer tomorrow or the next day. It could take months before I would respond. (Look at the "answer"—)

Aha. You see that what I want now is not an answer for the roshi. I want to become free. When I am, that will be his answer. For, in part, when I am free I am responsible to on one; hence I am totally responsible. There is the natural ethics in this work again. However, the point is that I am not working for an answer or for the roshi. I am working for myself. When I am strong, the universe behind me, I will be free. That is, I will not have to go to sanzen.

A nice thing occurred during zazen last night. (Otherwise it went poorly. Pain, and the impression of formal zazen in company with others, are not for me.) I daydreamed that the roshi was getting angry at me and hitting me with a stick. Regular Walter Mitty stuff. Then I was able to say to him: "You see, you are not so hot." The occurrences were vivid. Then suddenly I saw that I did not hate the roshi but that a part of me does: my ego. But *I* do not. ——This is classical and according to theory, but I *experienced* it. The theory became real.

So I come to "I am I." One way of looking at this is as follows. A person has an ego and he is a self. A good deal of the time, especially when he is with other people, but also when he is with things, it is his ego that resopnds to the situation. That is, what he has been taught to be, trained to be, responds. Not his self. This happens more with other people than with things, because other people have egos too, and like responds to like. When you meet a person whose self responds, it is refreshing and often shocking, because each self is unique. (This is recognized in the use of proper names.) Now, "I am I" is the self crying out, if you will. It is an expression from the self, from what underlies convention. Since it underlies convention it underlies law; for convention is law, both the regular (called natural law) and the imposed regular (called civil and moral law). Hence, the sense in the doctrine of the freedom of the will.

But then, of course, one wants to ask: (*a*) what is this I, pointing to me; and (*b*) if it is free, will it not do anything whatsoever and get into trouble? If you try to answer (*a*) directly you will only get into difficulty. You have first to see that language, when it is alive, is metaphorical. Literally there is no ego and no I. To speak of them is just to point to an experience, which is to me now quite real. The answer to (*b*) is harder to see. I doubt whether it will do any good to say that a man is neither good nor evil but that he becomes so in society. However, it follows from this statement that the free self will never do anything that will get it into trouble, because it is "beyond good and evil." There are good and evil egos but not good and evil selves.

Next morning before sanzen   I am increasingly able to have the experience of my self and to see the workings of the ego, busy with thoughts and wishes. I am going in to tell the roshi that I am I. But look at the effort to accomplish something in *that! There is nothing to accomplish!*

Now that slips from the mind and I am calm, which I now find is the mark of what I am calling "I": calmness, tranquillity. Just concentrate on *mu* and go in with an empty mind.

Sitting quietly, the roshi listens.
"There is nothing to accomplish."
He looks up and straight into my eyes.
"No."
"Yes."
He smiles slightly:
"Not yet. *Mu.* You must concentrate. You must work on becoming *mu.* Get the whole universe behind you."
Bell.

Upon doing zazen immediately after this sanzen tears came to my eyes. A great emotion overwhelmed me. I should have cried had others not been in the zendo. For a brief moment I felt the whole universe behind me. It was deeply moving. I felt that I might lose consciousness. Then anxiety. Then depression (I had been so happy when I started out in the morning). I did not lose consciousness, but went on to feel as though I were going to faint. A little later I could see why one bowed to one's pillow, to the room, to the roshi. Thank you.

The effects of the experience remained during a subsequent conversation with the roshi and others, and for two hours thereafter. I was abstracted. I could stand the prattling of one of the conversationalists far more easily than usual. What is there to be disturbed about with such a one?

Will I lose all this that I have gained? It has been so short a time that I have come to it. Yet how can I lose what has been there all the time?

A religious experience? Okay. I prefer "finding myself" for all that is happening now.

Still, the element of duality remains. Is that why the roshi said, not yet?

My reaction was as much to looking into the roshi's eyes and feeling calm and being aware of it as to anything else.

Being alone now seems essential. That and the recognition (at least) that there *is* the self, to pursue this metaphor. It seems only right that the self can grow strong only in solitude. It is the ego that thrives on company. When the self gets strong it may be able to risk distraction, but at first it cannot stand it, I feel.

"Become your self" is another way of writing "become *mu*."

One walks a bit reverently as a self.

I think that for a brief flash I was at one with the universe this morning. What does this mean? Not that you are *literally one,* but that the ego is gone. Hence the term "universal mind" which bothers translators. It implies one stuff, no individuality. In fact it seems to be a description of being egoless. This shows how words can ensnare. Terms like "universal mind" used to ensnare me and produce revulsion, because taken literally (and

112

not transparently) they are nonsense. Any term is nonsense when it is not *used*.

In a way I can see that the ego is not evil or unnecessary as I have thought. It is a natural part of learning to control the body. Eating (as we do it) is just as much as habit laid on as is talking. Yes, talking is a habit too. And therefore social. Hence, the self has no language. Hence, too, the ineffable of the mystical, the self. And it is only mystical because it is private.

As I get surer of myself, *as I get stronger* (and there goes the duality), I will write less.

NOTES

1. See Chap. Three, n. 3.

2. Various people who practice meditation, or concentration, try to get the mind in different places: Zen Buddhists in the stomach, others in the heart, others in the center of the forehead, and so on. This suggests that the lotus position and the imagery of "the mind dropping down" are just techniques, not necessarily related to the process of transcending the logical and getting into the present.

3. One can put it any way. The use of quotation marks breaks down here. The use of quotation marks may have been instrumental in overcoming dualism. It may also reinforce dualism.

CHAPTER FIVE

My impression is that the koan work has entered a new phase. I feel that it has, and the roshi's remarks during sanzen indicate it. This does not mean that I will shortly get the answer to the koan. It might come at any time (I feel) and it might take years. However, I think all the rubbish has been cleared away and I am at the heart of the matter. It is also a mark of the new phase that I do not care now whether I get the answer. Or rather—since I do know it—whether I will be able to demonstrate it to the roshi. That is to say, I can leave Kyoto whenever I want.

In the case of Zen training, "doing philosophy" is trying to get *the* answer to a koan. Does the foregoing therefore mean that I will stop teaching philosophy? No, it means that I become a teacher with philosophy as the vehicle, so to speak.

Sitting quietly, the roshi listens.
"What does the 'mu' mean? Everything." Long pause. Then: "Not yet, not yet. Mu."
Bell.

That came about as follows. I felt the meaningless; that is, "Do not give an answer." Then I saw how I keep striving when I should not be (and understood how people can persist in asking meaningless questions—what *is* the meaning of life?). The thing (the answer) is to stop going to the roshi *and* to be

134

able to do so because I do not have to do so. Then I got a step deeper. The striving too is part of the ego. I had thought (just yesterday) that it was *I* striving to live. It is not. The striving is ego too. Why should the self strive? It has nothing to prove.

Very well, but what to do when I walk into sanzen? Bow and walk out after reciting the koan? Too logical. All right, I will say that the "mu" means everything (which it does). Then when he says that that is phenomena to (logic), I will reply: I know it. The point is to come out myself and show that I am present and not just my ego. Fence with him a bit to show that I am there and that I know it.

Now note that the reply was "not yet." Not "no," but "not yet," just as though the answer did not count but a state of affairs did. I have felt this, and now comes the 'not yet' several times.

Yet how does this jibe with X's report that he got his answer to his first koan one day while he was on the way to the bank?

Is this business that you have a self something to cling to so that you will not let go of the ego? I do not think so. I know that I am on the right track. What difference does it make if it is *the* right track? (*a*) None. (*b*) You know there is, *I* know there is no *the* right track. There is only your track. ——How about the way you now take egolessness (literally), and before as there being no substances? Is not the self a substance? Looks bad, does it not? But remember that this is all a psychological shift. The way that you *think* is changed. Not things as they are. There are still flowers. There is still Paul. He was born and he will die. I was and I will. The point still is: there is no *essence* that goes on forever. In this respect everything is related. If there were essences there would be separate things. Aha, the idealists' stuff on the internality of relations = no essences = Wittgenstein's: Look for the use, not the meaning! You escape the fear of death by accepting death. How can

135

¹¹⁹ you fear what you accept? And accepting death = accepting the interrelatedness of all things (since annihilation means no essence). Therefore, there is no self. There is I, Paul, this body, this mind, this man. So the self is not an entity which I have come across. It is perishable Paul. The talk of the self is just a way of getting at this. And the calm "self" is just Paul undisturbed by worries, wishes, plans, and so forth.

The foregoing is a conceptual advance. It must be felt, too. When I get so that I am no longer trying to prove anything to anyone, I will be strong.

Now, the self is Paul. Getting to know the self is not, therefore, mysterious. And other people do or can know us better than we do ourselves. For our egos get in the way. Of course, other people's egos can, too, so far as their seeing us is concerned.

Despite the foregoing about the self, I do have a sensation of hanging on to some *thing,* the self. All right. So what? I can also hang on to an iron bar, but this does not mean that it has an ¹²⁰ essence. Essences are creatures of "thought."

¹²¹ Still I come back ever to that thought of the answer to the koan. Despite where I am now I come back to it.

The doctrine of no-mind. That is, in a way, the answer to all koans. But what does *this,* the *mu,* koan say? Be empty. Be egoless. Be yourself. Be.

Might it not be the case that one can have the correct feeling, and then any word (as answer) will do? But how does this jibe with (*a*) the fact that all answers to koans are checked by finding or making up a poem which gives the point of the koan[1]; (*b*) the fact that *answers* to the koans can be published (some-¹²² one has threatened to do this); and (*c*) the fact that the koans are verbally different, that is, that their *Bedeutung* may be the same but their *Sinns* differ?[2]

Just being yourself = just being there, all there; that is, conscious too. Being conscious. (Note: not *of* yourself, but being conscious. Being conscious of yourself is being self-conscious.)

You say that you do not need an answer, but you do. Otherwise you would stop looking for one.

You see, you were right before in saying that you should concentrate on *mu*. But you were hung up on the word instead of into the thing! The big step, therefore, was from the word to the thing! The thing-*mu*! That is nondualism: to be with the things! Then words can be used! Otherwise you are stuck with meanings!

Sitting quietly, the roshi listens.

"The 'mu' means this and this and this," pointing to things and pounding them.

"Yes." Long pause. "But you have not yet transcended the opposites. Mu." As if to indicate concentration.

Here is another lecture which came out from remarks about his health during a conversation with a roshi this morning. He told me how well X is taking care of him. But X is not doing it for me, he said, X is doing it for my disciples. X tells me that my body is old and worn out, and is right. But I must go on teaching, so I obey X. That is Zen: knowing when to say "yes" and when to say "no"—when to kill and when to give life— when you have to do this and when you have to do that. You must be pliant and elastic. ——Then out came Aristotle's doctrine of the mean, although Aristotle was not referred to.

Still, you must be like an iron ball: firm, yet able to roll anywhere with your center always at your center. Remember the triangle, too. Don't be top-heavy. Do not waver.

(All this is clear and well known. It is an old teaching. What the saying of it made apparent was that the teaching is one thing and the realizing it another.)

The roshi went on to compare his work to that of a carpenter who makes a column from a block of wood. First you knock off the four edges, then you knock off the other edges which result, and so you keep on until you have the column.

(Not a bad metaphor. The koan is one of the tools, like a sword, which in the hands of the pupil guided by the teacher hacks away at the edges. However, the metaphor obscures the fact that there are tools and tools. Life itself knocks off edges, or can. Many old people are wise without formal instruction simply because they have lived. The roshi's lectures are tools, as well as the koan and his sanzen. But it is easy to get overimpressed with a particular tool. And it is easy to get overimpressed with a particular way of life without realizing that it is just your way.)

126 What about that not having transcended opposites? (The feeling is strong now that none of these people is enlightened. It is abetted by observing the cliquishness among the various Zen teachers and their adherents. Sure, I have come to some of the reality of Zen Buddhism in Japan, but it is still you who count, as old Rinzai said. Nor is this sour grapes due to not getting through in sanzen this morning. I know that I need to go a long way to kill the ego, and I had nevertheless regained that feeling this morning for the thing-*mu* which led to the answer: *mu* is everything—this and this and this.)

Now for transcending the opposites. I have gotten pretty well beyond words with my koan, but now what? (And you must be fair and remember the reports available of those who solved the *mu* koan. Great stuff, they said. They also said: to hell with the methods, with sitting, etc. And one roshi speaks only of passing a koan and nothing of satori. In the details, in 127 other words, one comes across great divergence.) First, it is possible that just getting beyond words is enough to give one man satori. Second, there is the—so to speak—physical matter of

138

overcoming the ego. That takes a long time. In other words, let us make distinctions (even though that is just logic). Here is one I have not made: there may be various causes of satori in various people. For example, one gets beyond words and has it. Another performs an egoless act and has it. These conditions are related to the doctrine of no-mind, but we overlook the fact that it has parts.

8

I feel this morning that I want to break out and *do* something. Swim. Travel. Whatever. I am also acutely aware of the fact that there are many ways of life. I pointed to things this morning and I am aware of them in a way in which I have not been before. It comes to this: how we *do* seek absolutes. And *now* I see how, despite getting to my self, etc., that is still what I have been doing. It is *true* that I have solved the koan when I quit doing sanzen. Just quit.

However, notice what you keep getting out of it. Maybe more will help? ——That is the ego talking.

You will learn more about the ego? What more is there to learn? Knowing *directly* that you *have* an ego is enough. Do they not after all speak of sudden enlightenment?

My answer to the roshi, my transcending opposites, therefore, is to quit sanzen. (Think how *hard* it would be!) Sanzen can be a crutch too.

How transcend? I have! Result? Do not go to sanzen, an act coming out of transcendence. An act on your own, *my* act. (Notice how hard it is. You can scarcely believe it.) If I waited and left sanzen under the force of circumstances, that would not be *my* act.

The great state of satori? Your reading about it has made you think that you should have it now. As it has made you look for visions. Want visions? Take mescaline. The great thing is to act on your own. This requires "the force of the universe behind you." Kill everything. Kill your sabbatical leave project, your months with a Zen master, etc., etc. ——*I* know that this act will not do this, but doubts keep entering. The only way to find out is to wait and see.

¹³⁴   The union of mind and body? This *act is* such a union.

¹³⁵   When I can stop doing philosophy whenever I want—
(I sat and thought for a moment. Misgivings. All kinds of doubts. No need to enumerate them.) I could easily quail. But I won't. (No need for an exclamation point there. You do not have to shout.) I could cry out for joy but I do not have to.

About death? You just die, that is all.

All the questions which the ego raises can be answered now.

I went and told the roshi and the advanced pupil who had introduced me to him that I was quitting sanzen. The act was done.

NOTES

1. Toward the end of his Zen study the student is asked to find or make up so-called capping verses for the koans he has passed.

2. See P. Wienpahl, "Frege's Sinn und Bedeutung," *Mind,* No. 236 (October, 1950). There it is argued that, roughly, the *Sinn* (sense) of a word or of a group of words is the combination of its physical properties in so far as it is an object or a group of objects which function as a word or words. The *Bedeutung* is the meaning or significance.

CHAPTER SIX

Reflections   Why should they have understood what has happened? It has happened in me. I have had no great religious or mystical experience. I have simply for the first time that I can remember done something deliberately and fully conscious on my own. An act of free will. And all the pieces of the puzzle have fallen into place. For example, no feelings of rancor, no Walter Mitty dream; I go on teaching, only now I teach students and not philosophy. So-called philosophy is just a method. One tries to free minds, your own as well as those of others. Meditation to continue? Yes. Quiet is important.

To quit studying Zen leaves a vacuum. It puts me on my own. This shows how this study, too, can become a crutch.

This is no *great* change but a positive step? I *told* myself that this is the answer to the koan? All right. The thing still is to stop whenever you want to.

Reactions: gaiety, lightheartedness, no fears, "I have done something real."

To say that philosophical questions are meaningless is true but thoroughly misleading. The same is true of: the riddle does not exist. For these are obviously real questions, they are asked. They are only pseudoquestions in an odd way. So it never does just to *say* that they are meaningless (and to accompany this with a theory), for to their askers they are fraught with meaning. A way of looking at them is: they are necessary for a man's spiritual development. If he does not ask them, how is he to become enlightened? (Necessary is a strong word; one might say that they are natural questions to this end.) So one must never *say* that they are meaningless, but let and help the student find his way through them. The koan technique in fact consists (looked at in one way) in confronting the pupil with philosophic questions and making him work his way through them. The only trouble with Western analytic philosophy now is that it is not enough, if at all, a part of the lives of men. They are not real philosophers, that is, but boys playing a game, albeit a good one. ——Of course the riddle exists. It is by seeing through it that one grows. The very fact that Wittgenstein said it does not is a sign that it had existed for him. He is misleading; or I have been misled, have misled myself, in reading him. ——The point here is: if you say that such questions are non-sense you may stop people asking them. Yet they are *a* way to wisdom.

How does one describe seeing a mountain without getting involved with the subject-object relation? Mountain seeing mountain? I see I? All is one? When you try to do what language cannot do *and* are stuck in language, you get non-sense. You have to break out of language somehow, perhaps by performing some act of free will. This shows me that Platonism, the conceptual barrier, is not due to the structure of a particular language, but to just using language at all. The Orientals are as much bothered by it as are Westerners. Russell's speculations in "Logical Atomism" (about the subject-predicate languages and their influence on metaphysics, the conceptual barrier) appear to have been in error.

The closeness of language to human experience is clearer now. To say such and such is just a conceptual mistake is misleading. Grief shows the connection between language and experience. A "conceptual" aberration is a living aberration. Changes in language are changes in human experience (the rational is the real). Meaningless questions are a search. Their outcome is different from that of asking ordinary questions.

This act has brought with it a desire to help others. Not do-gooding, but doing what I have been doing professionally with an awareness that that is what it is: teaching. It brings with it, this awareness of a simple fact, something like a sense of com-mitment or duty. For it is a fact that teaching helps others, even if we do it in order to feel good or for some other "bad" "motive."

Did I solve my koan? Of course. But so does *solve* get looser yet.

What came, has come, over me? Enlightenment? Who knows? But a great change. One can arrest the process when one chooses.

Reflections a day later   Doubts. I do not *really* have the answer to the koan. What makes me think that I would have it if I quit sanzen, or working on the koan? Yet it is plain as a pike-staff. I know what "mu" means. I know why Joshu said it. What was needed was an act. And whatever else it may be, it has made an enormous difference to my life.

Of course, much remains to be done. One does not become like the triangle over night. Training must continue, and even some sanzen might be included.

Is this only a stage on the first koan? Ah, the trap again! Doubts again. Consolidate your step. So it is and is not a stage —another reason for there being many koans. Once you are on your way you can do it more and more alone. However, don't lose sight of the first real step. Continuity, yet suddenness too.

I had thought that philosophy in the Western sense was completely foreign to Orientals. It turns out that it is not. From this one sees that the parallel between Zen and Witt-genstein is close. Rinzai Zen Buddhism is in one sense simply a method for undercutting intellectualism and conceptualism and getting through to radical empiricism. The limits of empiricism are mysticism. Zen Buddhism is not mysticism, it is radical empiricism.

Things are egoless = look for the use, not the meaning.

And there are *uses,* not *a* use.

When I speak of the soul now I do not mean an entity. It is a way of talking and points to a certain experience, my experience now. Otherwise you look for the meaning instead of the use of the term.

Doing philosophy like this is all right. It is not all right when you get stuck with the meaning. What is the meaning of life, say. Then you have to break through to life.

The fact that egolessness may be seen to equal "look for the use, not the meaning" suggests how profound Wittgenstein was. Also, seeing that language is part of the spiritual life of man reveals the profundity and "religious" character of his work.

I sit in my room now, content just to sit.

A day later   However, the reflections must be interrupted. It transpires that one does not do things only in the way one thinks they are done. From two of the roshi's advanced students I learn or infer the following.

a. One does not tell a roshi that one is quitting sanzen, simply because that is not done in Japan. In this case you work through your intermediary. This also leaves the door open in case you might want to return.

b. You can stop or start sanzen whenever you want; that is, roughly, given protocol it is up to you.

c. The koan process is for the purpose of producing the Buddha state or the state of no-mind, samadhi. It is not to produce enlightenment (satori) unless the other is what you mean by that term. It is a lengthy process. (Clearly I have not achieved anything like samadhi.)

d. Even when you have "passed" the *mu* koan, you come back to it and work on it from time to time.

e. People often want to quit sanzen. That is when monks have to be dragged into these interviews. The desire to quit springs from the ego you are trying to control fighting back. ——(Interesting that they should use my language about the ego.) I replied to this that it was just the reverse with me. The ego wanted to continue sanzen. *I* wanted to stop.

Out of this came two matters of interest: (*i*) I went on to say that I wanted to consolidate on my own the taking of my first free step. To which the reply was: "You are, in other words, ready for your next koan." There is no problem about the answer to the first koan of *mu*. It is given to you. But the roshi will keep you at it and keep you at it, to get you deeper into your own mind, closer to samadhi. Furthermore, it is one of the deepest koans and you often come back to it. (*ii*) In the talk of the passing of a koan no mention was made of satori. I infer from this that the term may have been overused in Western literature on Zen Buddhism.

f. A mark of a man can be that he speak of *his* Zen. Zen can be compared to a liquid in a vessel. We are but the containers. The container may be leaky and dirty (corruption in the temples at various times), but the liquid cannot be tampered with without being lost. Anyone who has tried to do so has collapsed and failed, or his work has.

The training is essential, so the temples have been essential. This is a reason why a lay line of Zen Buddhism is almost doomed to failure. Another is: a layman tries to develop *his* Zen. His ego interferes. The temple and the discipline are maddening, but they help to keep the ego out of the training. In the training the pupil learns to do things simply, he learns reverence for things (for example, water, by being allowed little of it).

145

g. There was talk of the enormous intricacy and artistry in a koan. Even if it never helped you to get in touch with your own mind, samadhi, it provides by its marvellous subtlety an aesthetic pleasure which nothing else can.

Reflections   In a way it is true that Zen is a liquid handed down in human vessels. It is also true that each person has his own life to lead. I guess we have to accept both.

It is clear that I have been hung up in the word satori. I have stuck too close to what one man has said with it. It may refer to an awakening, to a feeling of oneness, to the feeling one gets when one encounters the I, to the feeling one gets when one performs a free act, and possibly to other things.

The koan work and my present stage in it go more into perspective. Sanzen should continue: (*a*) for the subtlety of the koans, and (*b*) to approach samadhi, a special condition of the mind. On the other hand, I have reached the "discovery which gives peace": I can stop doing philosophy whenever I want to. Stopping sanzen is a sign of this. I could start sanzen again for reasons (*a*) and (*b*). I cannot do it in order to find the *key* or satori because of the solution to *the* philosophic problem and because of the free act. I might come back to sanzen after the results of the free act are fully entrenched.

(I had better tell X to leave that door to the roshi open.)

Do not copy Wittgenstein. Yes, but one can see a pattern here. And *that* puts a new light on the matter of the Zen Buddhists following an absolute. Do not get caught up in that word, either! Stick to the facts, to experience. If experience leds this way, follow it. Why? Remember about listening.

He who is stuck is he who will not listen. (So I should have listened to X about keeping the door open.) There are times, however, when one talks and does not listen: when he has trod the path and can help another who is stumbling to find it.

147

148

So you have your cake and eat it too: you fortify the free act and continue sanzen. Why? Because you have solved the philosophic problem, seen the civil status of a contradiction. That leaves you with deepening the calm. After the philosophic problem is solved there is you. Might that not be why it was said that I was ready for the next koan? *Mu* solved the philosophic problem, but I am still left, and *mu* can help on that. That's it!

Now, is this falling back into the trap? It is and it isn't. It is, because taking on another koan is *in a way* doing philosophy again. It is not, because taking on another is working more and more to strengthen me. Doing philosophy on a deeper level, if you will—something that is different in a way from what has gone on before. A whole new phase is beginning.

So "mu" means *mu*. You keep on only to get more into yourself.

The next step: to be strong enough to go back to sanzen? Aha! *The next step*: to be able to take it or leave it; that is, to make a free choice; this is, to be on your own.

All this will teach you to get cocky over *one* act of free will.

Next day   You give up philosophy to come back to it (the second free step). This only sounds paradoxical. For I had first to give up philosophic questions (as meaningless) in order to come back to them to *use* them, in self-analysis. Or, not so much self-analysis either, as in releasing myself. Knowing the self is knowing it *directly;* it does not involve analysis, so to speak. The "analysis" is the process of uncovering the self and freeing it, clearing away the debris of the ego. But the self is not analyzed, unless one means by self the combination of the ego and the I. The whole unit is analyzed, cut open to let the self emerge. But it needs no analysis. Indeed, being a unit or pure, it is unanalyzable. Hence, analytic power is all right for the so-called relative world. But for the "absolute" world of the self, only the intuitive faculty is needed. Just to "look."

So one stops doing philosophy and one does not. One stops asking meaningless questions and one does not. One *does* stop looking for their meaning and looks for their use, or rather uses. Thus can I go freely back to sanzen.

You cannot successfully describe all this or justify what you do say, because something has happened to *you*. You change. That is part of it, nor is the change visible. Therefore, unless someone does it himself he will not believe you. And you cannot put yourself into words, any more than you can put any thing into words. Words can be put into words. That is all.

Now I can see how men can go away from sanzen and come back to it. You can take it or leave it and use it when you have a chance. To drive yourself to use it would be an ego act. Driving is from the ego, that is, from the outside. Therefore I am, and can be as a whole man, calm.

Is this talk of the I and the ego schizophrenic? No. It is instrumental. To what? Self-possession (a nice word which I had not noticed before). The same may be said of the notion of samadhi (the mind meditating on itself) which seems to contradict the notions of no-mind and egolessness. The contradictions are only apparent and not real, because these terms are ways of talking to bring about something and are not part of a theoretical formulation.

And so you can keep on meditating, or stop it at will. If a thing is to be used you can take it or leave it. Otherwise it gets a hold on you.

About the true self of which I speak so much now, I wish I could be more precise, that is, helpful. The following isolated remarks may be of some use.

It is more an experience or a series of them than a thing.

It is a characteristic of koan work that it has about it none of the *emotional* throes which one associates with, say, psycho-analysis, or Christian suffering. Why should cutting through to the self be emotional? Why should the self be emotional? I broke off with the roshi and now I am going back. The work is neuter. This conveys some of the feeling.[1]

Enlightenment for the West means a surface phenomenon (or it did for me), an intellectual one. Yet it is a deep thing. It is deep because it takes a long time and because it is not simply an affair of intellectual or conceptual or ordinary thought. Yet it is not deep, for it is a direct awareness of the self. It does not require analysis in most of the usual senses of this term.

Of the self or soul or whatever you call it an advanced Zen student said to me: Do not worry about where it comes from or what it is for. There it is as an experience. Think of being hit with an arrow and bleeding. One does not wonder where the arrow came from and who shot it. One thinks of the bleeding and deals with it.

This student talks of "it" as the mind and says that it is always on the go. It never stops with one experience. If we do, as I started to with my first free act, and latch on to the experience, we "lose" our mind, for it moves on. ——This suggests that being yourself is being in the immediate present all the time. You are at the intersection of space and time. It has taken much to produce you, but the present moment here is what is real. Live in it. See how this fits with the talk about concentration and makes somewhat less of an effort of it? The "aim" is to be able to be in the here and now at this very moment and only in this spot. That is to be egoless. The ego is spread out, diffuse. The experience of the present moment always at the present moment is the experience of the self.

The student also said that Zen students do not worry about satori, or getting it, whatever it may be. If you suddenly see a thing as you have not seen it before, a little more clearly perhaps;

or, if you suddenly feel contact with a person, and credit these to your zen "work," all right. "We call them by-products of the process." But do not aim for them. Aim at being the mind, being the self (that is, at this moment in this place).[2]

——This is to be *all there*. You do not have to talk of overcoming dualism, etc., etc., although you can if it helps to lead you to this experience.

This experience may also be described as "a feeling of calm." The process is settling into a feeling of calm.[3]

Sitting quietly, the roshi listens.

"The 'mu' means nothing."

This produces a long discourse, the substance of which is:

The last time, you said it meant this and this and this. You have to transcend yourself, give up yourself. You remember Christ? He died and rose again. You have to do that. That is a very good explanation.

When I went to the roshi and told him I was quitting sanzen, and that that was the answer to the koan, I thought this was *the* climax of the work. I did not recognize, what I should have known, that there is only one final climax. And that when it occurs one does not know it. It is odd how blind we can be to the simple fact of death and what it means to us. We think without realizing it that we will live forever. At least I have just learned that I have been "thinking" this way and that I probably will, without knowing it, for some time.

And yet *a* climax did occur, although I see now that it did not occur just when and in just the form in which I thought it happened. I thought it occurred when I performed the first consciously free action of going and telling the roshi that I was through with his "course," and that this action was the answer to the problem he had posed. I was free. For a few hours I was completely free. I had taken a step on my own.

It took forty-eight hours for me to see that I had only stepped into further bondage. For by then it had become a principle not to see the roshi. And secretly in my heart I lorded it over those who continued to see him. Whereupon I took a second step. And this was why the first one was good: it made possible the second and gave me the strength to make it. This was to accept the fact that I could see the roshi or not see him. Neither shun him nor cultivate him. So this morning I saw him again.

And that is the full climax. Something died and I was reborn. Two acts, not one. Therein lies the meaning of death. But I do not understand it. I have the words for it, but I do not stand under them. Their light is not on me. I still stand in the shadows.

So I have no idea where to go next with *mu*. It is clear from the foregoing, which is a response to the roshi's remarks this morning, how far I have to go toward accepting death. For I do not see how one can be reborn from the final death.

Possibly it is: accepting that one is not.

However, it seems now that to do this, and thus answer the *mu* koan, you would have to go through a series of "deaths" like the one just described.

But I do seem at a standstill now, a real gap.

On looking into *The Middle Way,* the Buddhist Society quarterly, I was struck by the fact that the writing, though verisimilar, seems to me—where I am—very much on the surface and typically intellectual. Thus I realize that my koan work is too intellectual. If I am going to listen, I must also listen to the advice to do more zazen, more of the physical.

Also, these Western "Buddhists" confuse the subjective and spiritual with emotion. This relates to the unemotional character, the neuter character, of the koan work. As noted above (n. 1 of this chapter), this is seen in Zen gardens. They are austere, the opposite of lush. One takes this as rigor and simplicity. It is also subjective and spiritual. It is both right and wrong to say that there is no language of the inner (*subjective* is also a misleading word). Right, because this recognizes the difference between the inner and the outer (the objective). Wrong, because there is a language of the inner: these gardens; and indeed any simple, severe, unemotional verbal language that is not simply practical.

Know thyself? The self is not what I thought it was. It is the "pure" thing buried under the ego. It requires no analysis. However, in work like the koan work something a little like analysis goes on: a hewing away of the ego to reveal the self. And when the self is felt (seen) then the ego becomes clear by simple contrast, or the fact that you can now look at it whereas you could not before.

This makes psychoanalysis ego analysis.[4]

"You cannot know your world until you know yourself." Of course *you* cannot because you are buried under your ego until you know yourself. It is your ego that "knows" the world before this. Its "knowing" is that of interpretation, making things as it wants them. Know thyself = direct awareness of the self, not "know" in the usual sense of ratiocinative knowledge.

What about the self and emotions? So far it has appeared that the self is "pure." However, this seems to make it impersonal and negative. How would the man who is aware of his self (and thus is a self) behave if he lost his child? Would he not suffer? An answer seems to be that a self enjoys itself and suffers, but does not drag others into it as would the ego, which is a man's social part. Its emotions would be private; those of the ego are public. Thus, two marks of a self are: (*a*) it is conscious of itself, and (*b*) its emotions are private. This suggests that not only is *I* ambiguous, but so are words like *emotion* and all the words for emotions. (The matter is reminiscent of Spinoza's distinction between the active and the passive emotions.)

It helps to remember that material like the foregoing is instrumental in bringing about the condition of calmness for which one also strives in zazen. Writing and thinking it is indeed a form of zazen. The stuff is not intended as a theory about human nature. It is not explanatory.

The notion that all explanation is instrumental is related to seeing that the so-called teachings of the Buddha, say, are vehicles (to be abandoned when they have done their job). By this means one sees the connection between John Dewey and Zen Buddhism.

Enlightenment as I used to use it was a misleading (because intellectualistic) term. It is not so much a matter of enlightenment as it is a matter of letting the self come through.

Once again, can the self suffer? Again I feel, no. It helps to see the question as follows. Can a man suffer? Yes. Even a self-aware man? Yes, because *self* and *ego* are just two ways of speaking. In fact there is no distinction between the ego and the self. Neither are entities. A man is a man. In a way the self and the ego are ways of behaving and experiencing. So a man can suffer. However, "that part" of him which is the self cannot suffer, for in that kind of experience there is no loss or gain. The self cannot lose anything or gain anything. So "it" cannot suffer.

How does one make a free decision (a decision by the self, in that language)? For example, suppose I am faced with the possibility of taking a trip, and my wife exhibits violent opposition to my going, how do I decide what to do? One waits to see how things develop. If they develop one way, I go. If they develop another, I do not go. It is important in this to be aware that one does not have to go *or* to stay.

But then how does one decide? One goes along with the

situation; that is, one does not *decide*. Decisions are mainly ego affairs. "In affairs of the self one does not decide." Thus, another term turns out to be "ego-self" ambiguous.

The matter must be carried a little further. In making a free decision a person goes along with things, playing it by ear so to speak. He sees that, when he thinks about the matter (the trip) in order to make a decision, he can find good reasons for going and good reasons for staying. He sees, that is, how thinking (in this sort of affair at least) is rationalization. He sees that, if you want to decide rationally, you have to get evidence and not think. Getting evidence involves waiting to see what happens.

One can see from this that there are *decisions,* there is not decision. And to see this is a way of understanding egolessness, or rather, a way of getting the feel of it. For, in point of fact, there are neither egos nor egolessness. Remember "transcend the opposites."

For the next fourteen days I traveled on a vacation from the Zen studies which had been arranged before the opportunity arose to do sanzen and when I was working on Zen Buddhism by performing zazen and reading.[5] The work on the koan consequently took on a peculiar aspect. There were no interviews with the roshi. I did some informal zazen each day. I found that conversations and certain reading were helpful with work on the koan, but that I made little progress with it without sanzen.

I also noticed at this time that a variety of factors can be employed in zen study, provided one is aware that they can be used for this purpose. I refer to conversations, reading, various contacts with other people, walks, etc. It is, in other words, a kind of study which involves the whole individual.

During the entire two weeks I was convinced that I had a

self or a soul, and that it was the calm that I felt. There follow
notes on a conversation and some reading which, either at the
time they occurred or subsequently, influenced work on the
koan.

   In a conversation with a Japanese professor of philosophy
he remarked, apropos of Zen Buddhism (he was not a Zen
Buddhist) that he used a koan from time to time to quiet him
or "to settle a situation." I suggested that working on a koan
was working beyond the positivists on the meaningless question
issue. I saw because of my second step how far that work goes.
(*a*) You not only get to the thing emptiness (instead of just
saying that questions are meaningless). (*b*) You use these
questions to get to yourself and to fight the ego. (*c*) And then
you see that they turn out to have sensible answers; that is,
that they are not meaningless. One might say that empirically
verifiable propositions lead to objective reality; meaningless
propositions lead to subjective reality or to the self *if used*. To
say that they are empirically meaningless is a good step. To drop
it at that is misleading. One might even say that propositions
"about" the subjective and some meaningless propositions *are*
verifiable. Talk of the soul and free will is. It is not empirically
verifiable in the usual sense, that is all. You cannot set up an
objective experiment to verify them. But I suspect that you can
set up a subjective experiment; for example, have a man
seriously work on a koan.

From reading   Dogen, thirteenth-century Zen teacher and
founder of the Soto sect, emphasized zazen and the doing of
quiet, good acts as the core of zen study. He taught that the
Way is attained through the body because of the unity of mind
and body. The law of the Buddha is that mind and body were
originally one; essence and form are not two.[6]
   For Dogen the mental attitude in zazen is one of detach-

ment and purposelessness. Do not await a great enlightenment; that is to be purposeful. The present moment in sitting
(meditation) is what counts. One has all that one needs then.
Thus, enlightenment and practice are one.[7]

Dogen on how one thinks during zazen: Do not try to keep
thoughts out. Let them come, but note them and then put
them to one side. Do not become attached either to thinking or
to not-thinking; or, one might say, the ideas thereof. Do not
become attached to the idea of Zen Buddhism either.

Dogen distinguished primal or original enlightenment and
acquired enlightenment. Hence, too, he saw practice and enlightenment as one. (This is like saying that we have a mind
which is pure at birth and all we have to do is to return to it.
It sounds like what I have been saying recently in sociological
terms.) Dogen also thought that practice and enlightenment
are one because, if the practice has a goal (enlightenment) then
in it you are attached. That is, "practice and enlightenment are
one" says the same as, or is deducible from, "be detached."[8]

Dogen did not give up koan study entirely, but regarded it
as secondary. For him the wonderful world of which the
Buddha spoke was the ordinary world.

A second unity for Dogen was that of the phenomenal and
the absolute world, hence of time and being. For him it seemed
that *being is* becoming. (I find this excellent if taken instru-
mentally, though it has the ring of an ontological statement).
From this it follows that the present moment is all there is.

In Bankei (1620) there is the example of a man who seemed
to regard enlightenment as simply a calm heart. For him zazen
could go on all the time, not just when one was sitting in the
zendo, and when it did you were enlightened. (How far this
is from all the emphasis on satori!)

Hakuin (1685–1768) is the father of modern Rinzai Zen. He
reports his work on the *mu* koan in his *Orategama* and in his

autobiography. He speaks of the enormous build-up of tension before he saw through the koan. When he did, he felt that he could see all the Zen masters of history standing before him. He felt wonderfully free and wrote some verse. This he took to his teacher and told of his experience. The teacher said of the verses: "This you have learned, this is your theoretical knowledge. Show me your enlightenment." And held out his right hand. Hakuin refused to believe this rejection of his enlightenment. An argument followed which was ended by the teacher twisting Hakuin's nose and saying: "You poor child of the devil, in the dark dungeon!" When Hakuin asked how he had failed, the teacher, Etau, gave him the koanlike story of the death of the teacher Nany Ch'uan. Hakuin worked on this and finally brought more verses on enlightenment. Etau said: "Confusion and nonsense." Hakuin replied the same. Whereupon Etau hit him twenty times, threw him off the veranda, and laughed: "You poor child of the devil, in the dark dungeon!"

In his autobiography, *Itsu-made-gusa,* Hakuin gives the sequel. He had almost decided to quit Etau when he went begging one day. An angry woman knocked him down with a broom for begging. Thereupon he got to the bottom of the koan. He returned to Etau laughing and full of joy. This time Etau stroked him with his fan and told him to pursue his enlightenment and never again called him a devil.[9]

In the *O1tegama* Hakuin apparently indicates that he had sudden and full enlightenment. His autobiography belies this. There he reports, not only the sequel to his work on the *mu* koan given above, but also later and deeper experiences, some of which came by reading a verse. He speaks, too, of six or seven great enlightenments and innumerable smaller ones which he got from hearing the snow fall and in other experiences of nature. One started as a dream from which he awakened. In another he saw different answers to all the koans from those which he had seen before. One of his greatest experiences came when he was forty-two, while reading the *Lotus Sutra*. He claims that he then saw the error of all his earlier greater or lesser enlightenments.

Hakuin accepted other methods for achieving the monism of Buddhism, such as the reciting of the *Nembutsu,* but he praised zazen and the koan exercise above all others. He also said that the amount of enlightenment is proportional to the amount of doubt that precedes it.

Back from vacation and preparing to resume sanzen, I realized that in the sanzen interview before the last I had said that the "mu" means this and this and this (pointing); that is, every *thing* or any *thing*. And in the last sanzen interview before vacation I had said that the "mu" means nothing. On alternate days, in other words, I had said that the "mu" means: (*a*) existence and (*b*) nonexistence. The roshi had said at the first interview: You have to transcend existence and non-existence. So—

Sitting quietly, the roshi listens.
"What does the 'mu' mean? I do not know."
159   "Mu."
As though to say: you have to work.

NOTES

1. One sees this characteristic in Zen gardens, which are the reverse of lush. However, perhaps *emotion* and *emotional* are not the right words here. Certainly many of the experiences one has during zen study are profoundly moving and might be described as emotional. However, they are also unsentimental and impersonal.

"Neuter" is a good term here. It may help to suggest that one think of nature in this connection. There are storms and cataclysms in nature, as well as an overall and abiding calm, yet one would not describe nature as emotional.

2. This man said in this connection that the roshi speaks often of "the big death." He suggested that my first step was a little example and that coming back to sanzen is like a resurrection.

3. It has been said that the Buddha's eightfold path is a *description* of the steps in the process.

4. See n. 2, Chap. Three.

5. Once sanzen started I gave up reading entirely. This at first appeared to me essential to that kind of study, then I became sure that it was. It was a move away from concepts. By the time I went on the vacation I had reached a point where I could read or not, as I chose.

6. I sense in this more clearly the importance of action, and that what has been lacking in modern Western attempts to overcome dualism is some bodily practice. Think of all the papers one reads on mind-body dualism and the talk of the mind-body problem. Then think of getting through the problem with action, dissolving it.

7. This statement, which I find most helpful, shows how reading and conversations can be used in zen study: they provide images which can be used in meditation to bring about calm and concentration. They sound like theories, but may be used as descriptions of the condition toward which one is working.

8. Dogen sought to simplify zen study by reducing it to zazen, which, it seems, anyone can do. In the history of Buddhism in Japan there was a wave of such attempts at simplification of the method in the thirteenth century, most of them going much farther than Dogen. It was a sort of popularizing of Buddhism—the beginning of the end. The popularizers overlooked Spinoza's insight: all things worthwhile are as difficult as they are rare. Simplify the method and you "simplify" the results, that is, dilute them.

9. Notice the process of deepening the enlightenment. As Eliot reports Hakuin's work on the *mu* koan, one gets the impression of a sudden and final experience. The present material comes from H. Doumulin, S.J., "Zen, Its Form and History," which I saw in typescript.

CHAPTER SEVEN

THE WORK FROM NOW ON UNTIL I INDICATE OTHERWISE OCCURRED during a sesshin (see Appendix); that is, during a period of a week in which I did nothing but zazen and two sanzen interviews a day. Heretofore I had studied zen as a civilian, so to speak: now I studied it as a militant. I left my lodgings and entered a temple.

The days and nights ran as follows. I include these details because they are a part of the work. My routine differed slightly from the monks for a reason which will become apparent. At 3 A.M. we were awakened by the sound of a gong. We rose instantly, put away the mosquito netting and our futons, washed hands and faces, and assumed a kneeling position in the zendo where we had been sleeping ("do" means house or building, "zen" means meditation). At the sound of a bell we then walked to the adjoining hondo (lecture hall). There till a quarter to four the monks and their roshi (the abbot) chanted sutras in a kneeling or lotus position. Then back to the zendo where we (except me because I cannot) assumed the lotus position until twenty minutes to five. During this time the monks had sanzen with their roshi. I could not because my roshi's temple was two miles away.

At twenty minutes to five a bell, and we walk to the mess hall. More sutras for five minutes, sitting cross-legged. Breakfast in complete silence: rice and pickles. At five minutes to five we walk back to the zendo and are dismissed with tea.[1] At this time the monks have a break until five-thirty when they resume zazen till seven-thirty. I instead walk to sanzen with my roshi. After that I walk back, and "meditate" as I go.

At seven-thirty we don working clothes and work till ten-thirty, picking weeds and cleaning the temple buildings. This was varied one morning by practice sutra chanting and a lecture by the abbot.

Lunch at a quarter to eleven. Rice, pickles, and soup with bean curd. From eleven to twelve-thirty the monks are off, in theory to meditate on their own. For my part I walk back for my second sanzen interview. From twelve-thirty until two-thirty the monks do formal zazen and have their second sanzen for the day. By dawdling on the way back I save my legs from further zazen. From two-thirty to four-thirty more work. At a quarter to five medicinal meal, as Buddhists are not supposed to eat after noon. Rice and pickles.

From five to five-thirty, bath. From five-thirty to six-thirty, "free" zazen. However, everyone lies around and talks. (In theory there is no talking during a sesshin except at sanzen. Orders are given by bells and gongs, and by the routine of the whole thing. Every effort is supposed to be directed to meditation, even during the work hours.) From six-thirty to ten formal meditation in the zendo, with five-minute breaks at the half hours. During this time the monks have their third sanzen for the day.

At ten, lights out. From ten to eleven everyone takes a pillow out into the garden for more free meditation. If you so desire you can meditate all night, and enthusiasts do. But you cannot go back to the zendo to sleep until eleven. In our case there were no enthusiasts, and we were all back on our futons at eleven. At 3 A.M.—

During sesshin I accomplished completely something to which I had only approximated during previous koan exercise: no reading or writing of any sort, and during some days no talking except at sanzen. I think this accounts in some considerable part for the results achieved during this week. For the rest, the results are due to the increase in zazen, in sanzen, and to the many details of life in the temple.

Sitting quietly, the roshi listens.

"The 'mu' means nothing."

"Who says this?"

"I do."

"There is an old saying in German philosophy: Was ist das Ich? That is the question. ——You must get beyond opposites. A while ago you said that the *mu* is everything. Now you say that it is nothing. Your wife is your opposite. You must get beyond. Was ist das Ich?"

Bell.

As I leave he calls me back:

"Notice that it is *das* Ich, not *der* or *die*. No opposites."[2]

On the walk back I was at first deeply puzzled. What sort of nonsense is this old-style German metaphysics?

But it isn't!

The I is reality! (A great feeling. For minutes I was absorbed in this.)

And *now* I understand death! When "I" die I just melt back into reality. Or better, there is no I. "I" is just a manner of speaking.

(I find myself drowning. My friend is frantically trying to reach me in the water. But I am calm. "He does not understand. He is on the other side." I am just going back, *melting* into what I have always been, in a way.)

Death is no problem when you see that you are reality, that there is no you.

And *now* I see through the concept of the self (I). There is no self! I have been mistaken. There is only an ego (emotions and whatever the psychoanalysts and the psychologists deal with).

(Once more, profound feeling. I am melting into the ground. I am one with it.)

Dying is no problem because there is no self to be destroyed. Of course the calm man suffers. Only reality does not suffer, except in so far as the calm man is part of reality.

161   I will say that the "mu" means nothing at the next sanzen.

Sitting quietly, the roshi listens.

"The 'mu' means no or nothing, depending on how you translate it."

"That is pretty good!" Broad smile. "But you are too much the philosopher. You deal always with becoming. Delve deeper. You have not had a samadhi yet."

Bell.

Of course it means nothing. Get clear beyond logic.

Sitting quietly, the roshi listens.

"There is a palm tree in your garden."

"You go too fast. Mu."

Bell.

Walking back I suddenly *see* what "mu" means. *Mu.* My God, it's as plain as a pikestaff! The "mu" means *mu.*

162
163   Finally the koan is talking to me. I am not thinking this. I have thought it before. I have not *seen* it before. The koan says
164   "mu" if you let it speak and do not interpret. I have been interpreting it all along.

The koan and I are one. I am saying the same thing it does.

I know (that) *mu* as (is) the answer. Even sentences can be known directly. Usually, however, we interpret. It is difficult not to do so. Even with things, we name or know them by name, and hence interpret.

> (Great elation. The earth is moving me. I am not moving on the earth. I am one with it. Tears.)

I know the answer. I have the answer.

Sitting quietly, the roshi listens.
"The 'mu' means *mu*."
"Now you have to go deeper. *Mu*. Work hard."
Bell.

Disappointment.
Yes, I had been expecting praise.
How shallow.
What will he say next?

Sitting quietly, the roshi listens.
"What does the 'mu' mean? Mu."
"You must work hard during zazen."
"That is difficult. My legs hurt so that I can't concentrate."
"Forget that. Strive to be calm."
Bell.

Walking back, I again have the experience of identification with the world. There is nothing to think about now. However, this time the identification is with a bamboo tree. Standing before it, I first have a brotherly feeling for it. Then I feel that it and I are one. I merge with it. It becomes conscious.

In zazen I sit through the pain. The agony is great, but I get dislocated from it. It occurs to me that I would have to do something like this if my son were to die.

Sitting quietly, the roshi listens.
"Mu."

165

He listens for a long time. Finally:
"A little. But go deeper."
Bell.

Then the roshi at sanzen began to speak of a great calm ocean into which I could get. (I was saying only "mu" after reciting the koan.) "Try to get there," he would say. I tried. By deliberately avoiding it I learned that all conversation dissipates calm. Nevertheless, my courage failed and I began to dread the long hours of zazen.

Once the roshi "listened" to me for a long time. Finally he said: "A little, but go deeper."

At the last sanzen during sesshin he asked me whether I had experienced the tranquil ocean.

"Fleetingly."

"You cannot maintain this state yet, but keep on working at it."

Reflections after sesshin   Certain results of this work stand out.

a. The self is reality; that is, the dissipation of the concept, self; that is, the loosening of its grip. To know thyself is, thus, to know reality; not conceptually but directly. Despite the previous observations about the talk of the self being metaphorical, and about *using* the word self, I had, underneath so to speak, thought of the self as an entity. An entity in me and contrasted 166 with the ego. ——The idea of the self is far more difficult to get free from than is the idea of the naming relation, although it is easier to see quickly the strength of the latter's hold.[3]

b. The by-products of these steps forward can be as vivid as has been claimed. They are experiences in which distinctions between subject and object, and between objects, disappear. They are experiences which make sense out of such propositions as: The one is all, all is mind. It might be said that such propositions are ways of expressing these experiences. They are not ontological claims; yet, when the distinction of subject and object is "forgotten" (transcended), it might be said that they are ontological.

c. Related to these experiences was that of finally letting the koan speak. This might be described as looking at it without any interpretation occurring, just seeing what the words themselves say. Interpretation may help to bring this about, but it is easy to mistake the interpretation for what it interprets. So a knowledge of Buddhism, its so-called philosophy and its history, may help one finally to "read" the *mu* koan (i. e., listen to it). The chances are, however, that this knowledge will be confused with the koan (the meaning of the koan, if you will). Thus, one will be led to say that the "mu" means: avoid concepts, be egoless, etc.

d. Learning of the calm ocean and seeing that speaking of it is a device for bringing about the state of calm.

e. By the end of the sesshin I felt how far I had to go with the main business: getting into the calm ocean.

f. Enlightenment and satori have been overplayed, or perhaps the words have unfortunate associations for Westerners. The ocean stuff, mastery of the ego instead of killing it, being the center of space and time, the triangle, tranquillity—all these strike me as better images.

g. The pain in sitting in zazen depends not only on improper physical balance but also on mental imbalance. For example, during the last night of sesshin I suffered little physical discomfort because (*i*) I was getting out the next day, and (*ii*) I had seen during the day how I built up tension by dreading the sitting, and how one can carry a pain about. (There is a story about two Zen monks who met a young woman at a stream. She could not cross without wetting her dress. To the horror of one monk, the other picked the girl up and carried her across. As

167

the monks went on their way, the one thought of their vows of chastity. After a while he could stand it no longer. He asked the other, "How could you have done that?" To which the other replied, "What! Are you still carrying that girl about? I put her down a mile back.")

Sitting quietly, the roshi listens.
"Mu."
"You've got to get to the ocean. Not yet."
Bell.

I am troubled with anticipations now, of meals, of going home, the end of the day. I cannot seem to sit in the present and quietly. I see how much I have always lived in the future.

Sitting quietly, the roshi listens.
"Mu."
He looks at my hands, then at my stomach, finally into my eyes.
"That is pretty good, but not good."

The calm ocean is the feeling of calm. When he first spoke of it I started looking for something inside me. There is nothing to look for. It is simply being calm. And you have it when you can think only of *mu* and feel it going all through you. Thinking of this helps to bring it about. And when you are calm there is less friction between you and the things about you than there often is. You behave as one does when, as we say, things are going well—except that you are aware of the strength there.

I have the impression now that I am swimming on the surface of the waters of Zen, taking occasional shallow dives.

The strength which is growing, however, does not come from Zen Buddhism. It comes from myself, that is, from reality.

A use of "mu": Does the dog have Buddha-nature? No. Am I a great philosopher? *Mu.* The "mu" cut off the ego. When one is calm one has no such delusions. One feels the melting into everything, the one is all; and this brings one into the here and now, the present moment, the everyday world. The past and the future turn out to be somehow unreal. No wonder "the problem of time" has obsessed philosophers and poets. Time is both real and unreal. It is also instructive to say that it is the measure of change.

To say that truth *is* reality sounds odd. Any description of a profound experience in abstract terms sounds odd. This is such a description.

Sitting quietly, the roshi listens.
"Mu."
Again he "listens" for a long time and this time appears disgusted.
"Mu. ——Remember the intersection of space and time."
Bell.

And so it goes. Up and down, but mostly up. Calm = being in the here and now, and this takes force.

Emptying the mind gets all of one into the here and now. As long as anything else mental is going on one is in the past or the future, just wandering.

I heard the *Muldava* played and a surge of warm feeling came over me. I felt far away from the effort, then, and a sense of warmth in another kind of life.

And so it seems that calmness is not enough. One has to "get to the other side," to a completely different way of thinking. This is difficult to put clearly. One senses it as one sees through ambition.

169

Japanese children are taught calligraphy as much to teach them composure as anything else. Composure, tranquillity, calmness. The same is to be learned from gardening, flower arranging, the tea ceremony. The principle is to get action out of negative action.

171

In this connection it might be said that the function of the koan is to produce a calm mind.

Is the mark of good calligraphy the reflection in it of the calmness of the calligrapher? The goal is not just calmness but action through calmness. Thus good calligraphy is vigorous.

In the study of Zen one retires (to master the ego) to return.

In Oriental painting a canvas is never full. A single branch or a bird is supposed to be all of nature. The void in these paintings is, to be sure, without color or form, but it is not without significance (function). It helps the picture to transcend the opposites of existence and nonexistence. So in action one transcends them by no-action which is action. Thus just sitting quietly and emptying the mind with *mu* is training for no-action because it is no-action.

Notice that there is no need for talk of the self when one puts it this way.

All the earlier talk about the ego and the self is part of the clearing of the mind, but I started to make it into a psychology and it began to use me. In the same way the "coming in contact with reality" stuff could be made into a theory, whereas it is just part of becoming calm, or egoless if you will.

When you say "calm" it makes it sound significant. When you say "egoless" it makes it sound profound and suggests metaphysics, which is a mistake. Thus the work I am doing is simple and not at all profound, although I keep trying to make it so. On the other hand, it is both simple and profound.

172

And what of metaphysics? There is none except talk, which leads to composure, which in turn is contact with reality. (This is positivism plus.) Of course there are no metaphysical *theories,* but there is finally the intuitive knowledge of reality. So you still have "knowledge" of ultimate reality as the old metaphysicians have sought it.

That being calm is being in touch with reality is a most important proposition. It takes the mystery out of the it.[4]

The whole point of sitting (meditation, zen) is to get beyond theories, to get into the here and now. It sounds silly when put so baldly, but this is it. This is how you get into the here and now: sitting. When you have seen this, all you have to do is to practice sitting to confirm the "sense" of the here and now. And to be beyond theories is to have a different way of thinking. This is connected with seeing how much philosophizing is theorizing, and that if you want reality you just have to plump quietly down into it.

Sitting quietly, the roshi listens.
"Mu."
The roshi draws the intersection of the X and Y coordinates with his right hand.
"You must be in the center and then get all around it." He makes a ball with his hands.

I should sit more.

Sitting quietly, the roshi listens.
"Mu."
"You have got to go deeper. More profound. Into your life."
He looks at me fixedly. "Mu."
Bell.
"Come back. ——Have I told you about your ancestors?"
"Yes."
"Think about them."

Sitting immediately after, I felt strongly for the hundred generations, how I was a product of them. I felt continuity with them and experienced the sensation I had when, earlier, I felt the power of the world behind me.

Later I saw that it was not just my here and now that counted. I was continuous in a sense with those hundred generations. I felt what was meant by going deeper. Of course it is I in the here and now, but it is also all the past and the future!

175

So I had made a step yesterday in seeing: just *going* to sanzen was part of "enlightenment." All is part of it if you are aware of it. Each moment. I do not walk there *for* sanzen, but the walking there is part of being enlightened; that is, of being calm.

And then I saw: being calm is being in the here and now, and vice versa. It is not just being quiescent. It is being in the here and now, and that takes effort.

This led to seeing: you do not have to stand still to be calm. Being calm is being knowingly in touch with reality (with some particular object). Nature is not "calm" (think of the storms), but nature is always nature; that is, it is always there, all there.

Then I realized: the foregoing is merely another step, it is not *it*. There is no *it*. There are steps.

So I had gone in to sanzen pretty much in the here and now.

And its effect was not only the powerful experience of identity with the past. It also led to the realization that consummations bother us (me) overmuch. To forget them is to live in and accept the present. Worry about death is a worry about a consummation. Freud is right that we seek death. Ultimately the interest in ends is an interest in death, the final consummation. Of course, the interest in ends also buttresses the denial of death.

Another way of meditating is to concentrate on being in the here and now. You can concentrate on *mu* or on breathing or on being in the here and now (by looking at some object, say).

Thinking about the ancestors does give "depth"; that is, it makes the present moment more concentrated somehow.

Sitting quietly, the roshi listens.
"Mu."
"You have to go deeper yet. Mu. This is pretty good. But you can go deeper."

This is getting to reality, and as you do, questions as to whether the past and the future are real disappear. All that matters is "getting into touch with the stuff," the trees, etc. Then you see that, of course, the past and the future exist *as you have always taken them to exist* before you raised philosophic questions. Indeed, nothing is changed except the person when he gets into (conscious) contact with reality.

The talk about the ancestors is, again, just instrumental. All that is real is the here and now. Meanwhile, of course, I did have a lot of ancestors.

Sitting quietly, the roshi listens.
"Mu!"
"Go forward," indicates penetration with his hand and: "The origin of life."

Yes, it is all very well. I can now imagine my mind in my stomach and this helps me to get into the here and now. However, there is another sensation often connected with doing this. It is a vague fear that my mind will actually, is actually, falling down. This induces an involuntary resistance to the occurrence. So there is some calm but no samadhi?

Sitting quietly, the roshi listens.
"Mu!" (Loud, forceful, but completely false; that is, deliberate. "I" was between the "mu" and myself.)
Bell.

It is silly to speak of the thing-*mu*, to treat "mu" as a noun. It is just the operation of negation. The character for "mu" == "not to have." Does the dog have Buddha-nature? He does not have it. On the other hand, there is the way in which the work on the koan has proceeded. If you treat "mu" logically you have Carnap's work. If you try to treat it somehow otherwise you have something like Heidegger's work.

What did Carnap get out of Heidegger's "Was Ist Metaphysic?" "Nothing." (An example of interpreting instead of listening.)

In thinking of the thing-*mu* I get egolessness, which leaves me with everything really except the idea of the self, or the illusion of the self. Finally, there are the ego and the self, in a manner of speaking (a manner of thinking), as Spinoza spoke of the passive and the active emotions.

No, I just have a long way to go in "controlling the ego," in "getting into conscious contact with reality," in "being calm," in "getting beyond theories." For this purpose I have the "mu." Herrigel had archery.[5]

It is in a way misleading to speak of the great death; for one does not kill the ego, one learns to control it. One does not abandon theories; one gets beyond them, learns to use them. What dies, perhaps, is a way of thought.

176

Have I become a Buddhist? A silly question. Buddhism is just one way to reality (to use that language). A method. To be

177

a *Buddhist* is to take the raft with you. To worry about the truth of any teaching is to get stuck on the way to reality. Have I found something of worth? A truth?

Is this *the* way? All such questions overlook the getting through to reality.

Here is a way of understanding concepts like no-mind, no-thought, thinking of no-thing (getting the hang of words like "no-mind," etc.): there is a custom of not speaking before sanzen in the morning. Now compare saying "Good morning" after sanzen with saying it first thing in the morning (right after sleep). It is in both cases the first verbal thing you do in a day, also the first social thing. Talk in sanzen is not really talk. It is talk which is not talk, not-talk. Of course it uses words, but that use is quite different from the ordinary. So is no-thinking "thinking." It is simply, so to speak, a different kind of thinking; thinking for a different purpose, if you will. Compare with the kinds of proof proper to scientific matters, legal matters, aesthetic matters. To say that the latter kind is not really proof at all is to stress its dissimilarities to scientific proof. It is also to overlook the similarities.

Sitting quietly, the roshi listens.
"Mu."
A pause, then he makes the intersection of space and time motion with his hand.
"Have you searched for that?"
"Yes."
"What did you find?"
????????
"I felt calm."
"Calm, eh?" He folds his hands and lowers his eyes. Then: "A little more. Muuuuuu."

Sitting later I felt well-balanced. "I can take it or leave it." And this felt good.

But what about that question of his: "What did I find?" Is that a koan? Should I have answered: "Mu"? "I"? "Nothing"?

Notice how work on the koan has stopped ever since I began saying "mu" every time, and is replaced by "work on the self." Now I do not think about the koan. I have no ideas about it. I am just trying to be *mu,* or be in the here and now, or be calm. The mind still wanders a lot, but these other things are becoming easier and last longer when they occur than formerly.

Nevertheless, I am still not far enough along to know whether I got another koan this morning, or to avoid speculating on the question whether I treat it as a koan.

I have thought lately about the roshi's saying, "You go too fast," when I ignored the koan and said, "There is a palm tree in your garden" (because I had noticed one as I went in for sanzen).[6] It seems to me now that, when I give forth with a successful "mu" (that is, when I am able at will to be in the here and now, or am *mu*), I could then go on to answer the koan by some irrelevancy. (It would not really be an irrelevancy, for it would be quite relevant to being egoless.) In a sense, then—or it is as if—I had gone on mentally to the next step but was not at the first step physically when I spoke of the palm tree; that is, I was not calm. And that seems to be what is now lacking in Western philosophy: the physical counterpart of the theory: the practice. One who believes that metaphysical questions are meaningless should himself *be* meaningless; that is, egoless. (Positivism is a philosophy with wider and deeper ramifications than one supposes at first sight of it.)

What I need now mainly, then, is meditation, for the body to catch up with the mind, so that they become one and dualism is thus overcome in my philosophical life.

Now, this is my own "philosophy." The result of my work is simply me in touch with reality; that is, a thing, not a theory. Hence the quotation marks around "philosophy," for I have no philosophy. I am just I, and whatever I write is simply a report. It might be used by someone for his own work. But the chances are against that, for it is not a skillful report.

Looking at contemporary philosophy from this angle, it seems that, after early positivism, pragmatism, and existentialism, baroque forms of these developed. Later philosophers wove

178

a subtle veil of words over the original realistic stuff. We are still waiting for another step to be made.

However, this remains: I need more zazen.

Sitting quietly, the roshi listens.
"Mu."
He looks at my hands for a long time. Then into my eyes.
Finally he shakes his head:
"That is pretty good, but not it."
Bell.

That worked, in so far as it did, because I had made a lot of effort prior to it in getting into the here and now, in being all there as I said, "Mu."

The Zen "study" is almost completely physical now. This helps me to see better why Herrigel's book could have been called *Zen in the Art of Archery.* What might be called the philosophical thoughts I now have are being used to get into the here and now.

The practice can be pursued wherever you are and whatever you are doing. Trying to "breathe" lying down, I saw how odd the talk is of "the mind dropping down." And it was harder to "get it into my stomach" in that position. Indeed, that seemed pointless.

When you "get through to reality" (to put it that way), you have little if anything to say. No theories spring to mind. You do not have the urge to say that this is the way things are, or that. Furthermore, one day while in this condition and looking at a boat, I clearly saw and felt how silly the question is: what are noumena like, what is the world really like? And how silly is the claim that there are noumena and phenomena (at least as an ontological claim—as part of awakening the matter is otherwise). All the common-sense explanations and views seemed right. And I saw how right Moore was (there were trees before men), though how futile his attempt was to get us to see this (his method). Do dogs see color? No, but we do. All right. That is the way perception occurs, and we know it. In other words I saw something clearly which sends epistemology and metaphysics by the board, except in so far as they are exercises in getting into direct touch with reality. This is "self-analysis" too, and it is what these studies were originally designed for: to know reality (it is misleading to say: to have a knowledge of reality, because of the "of").

Metaphysics, in other words, is not science, it is not theoretical. It aims at direct knowledge. On the other hand, it is like science in that the utterances of the metaphysician are to be used. The purposes in the two cases, however, are different. One uses the "sayings" (laws) of the scientist for control of the environment; of the metaphysician for control of the ego—i. e., for direct knowledge of reality. With this knowledge comes tranquillity and strength.

Both optimists and pessimists basically want to get rid of evil, each in his own way. Neither accepts reality as it is: as having both good and evil or neither, depending on how you look at it. These people, therefore, want something for nothing. This is to be out of touch with reality. Or, to put it otherwise, it is being immature, wanting to have your cake and eat it too. All the talk of understanding "the meaning of death" is this too. It is trying to get rid of death, which is a fact. ——On the other hand, of course, it is right to get free of the hold which the ideas of these things have on us.

Sitting quietly, the roshi listens.
"Mu."
"You went to the oceanside. What did you find there?"
"I don't understand."

"What did you find there? How was the ocean? How did it look?"

? ? ? ? ? ? ? ?

Then: "Calm inside, waves outside."

"You are big waves, I want you to find the calm."

Sitting later, I thought about the calm and how far I am from it. It is apparent that he could keep me on the *mu* koan indefinitely, for it will take a long period of more effort than I am making to achieve this calm.

A thought occurs frequently lately, especially when I hear Western classical music: a lot of what I am experiencing in the matter of calm is the Oriental way of life. And there are various ways of life. Of course, I wanted to get through to reality before I came here and have done that some, and there is a sense in which we are awfully busy in the West and have thereby lost contact with reality. Perhaps, therefore, I am noticing in this thought my tendency to seek an absolute and to think I am finding it in this way of calm.

The foregoing helps to show how one can get caught up in theories. What are the *facts?* That is the question. Or what are the experiences? And that is where sitting comes in. It is a way of getting to the facts.

All that is needed now is zazen.

Sitting quietly, the roshi listens.

"Mu."

Lengthy pause.

"Not yet. You have got to go much deeper into nothingness." He gestures down and exhales deeply. "You understand?"

Sitting later, I saw that I am making literally no effort now. Nor have I ever in this work. Of course, going to sanzen and doing the sitting I am is some effort. But what is indicated is a prolonged and *concentrated* effort. I know about "the other shore." A mark of that is that I can now read idealist and religious writings, and "illogical" things such as: The one is all. But to *be* on the other shore requires more effort than I am making. More quiet is needed, too. Honen's urge to become a hermit is understandable.

Is what I am at here the same as getting mastery of the ego? Not quite, and yet making the change real and mastering the ego might come to the same thing. Being rationally able to accept the irrational seems quite different from understanding the stuff about mastering the ego. Yet in a sense, rationally accepting the subjugation of the ego is accepting the illogical. How can you *be* a person by subjugating a person? Yet we get around the illogic here by using the notion of the ego. It is not the person we subjugate, it is the ego. ——Ah, no! It is the self, or rather the idea of the self, that we get through for the change. That is the "great death." That's it! ——The feeling of dissolving into the stuff from which I came. Descartes on distinctions, real and otherwise. Spinoza solved the problem of interaction by denying that there are any real distinctions. It is a step to the other shore to see and feel no real distinctions.

Sitting quietly, the roshi listens.
"Mu."
He listens. Then:
"A little more. Go forward."
Bell.

Seeing and feeling the "self" dissolve again produced this. I was calm when I went in to sanzen. I was in touch with reality.

Sitting later, the concept of the ego definitely went by the board. By this I mean (i. e., in other words), I saw clearly that it, too, is a manner of speaking. "Ego" is an instrument, not a name. This leaves me just as I find myself, with behavior stimulated from without (both from the past and from the future) and behavior which comes from within. ("We can be stimulated from the past." That is another way of talking "about" the ego.)

Now what about *das Ich?* It, too, goes by the board. There is no *Ich.* And so one is left with nothing (*mu*). That is, with everything. That is, with no concepts, except as tools. That is, with no *illusions.* For it is not that there are no concepts. It is the illusions we have about them, the hypostatizing of them, we seek to be rid of. There is nothing wrong with concepts. There is only something "wrong" with us.

"Making philosophical ideas real" = "learning to use them."

More about the getting in touch with reality feeling: it comes like a jolt and is like coming out of a daydream. Whatever is being looked at at the time comes into sharp focus.

Sitting quietly, the roshi listens.
"Mu."
A lengthy pause. Then, his face eager and alert:
"You must fill all space and time."
Bell.

Sitting later. "Fill all space and time." That is in a way the reverse of "you are at the intersection of space and time." And it includes the ancestors and progeny, and the power of the universe images. It makes evident the amount of effort needed to get into and stay in the here and now. (If you are in the here and now, you do "fill space and time.")

Repeat: "getting rid of (the idea of) the ego" is not getting *rid* of it, but coming to be able to *use* the idea. Ego psychology is left. It is a fine tool. It is just that I stop hypostatizing. I have known about this for a long time. The question is: how far do I *know* it?

You can take or leave sanzen, for example, or anything. When, therefore, do I stop sanzen? When I leave for home; that is, when the *circumstances* indicate one way or the other. ——That helps to "describe" the reality feeling.

Sitting quietly, the roshi listens.
"Mu."
"You have got to go to the boundaries. You have got to go to the boundaries of space and time."
Bell.

Does this mean to get beyond the concepts of space and time, too? Do I have to work on them too, as I did on the concept of the self? If so the *mu* koan seems never-ending. It is one thing to get beyond all concepts all at once and another to get beyond them one by one. But it seems that you have to do it one by one.

On the other hand, "beyond the boundaries of space and time" feels like a powerful image to use in meditation to bring about the calm.

It is a never-ending process. I keep wanting fulfillments, endings. It goes on forever. ——What does? Reality.

Sitting quietly, the roshi listens.
"Mu."
Pause.
"You have not got to the boundaries of space and time yet. Your *mu* is pretty good, but. . . ." He makes the intersection of the coordinates and says, "Space and time. Like this." He folds his hands, lowers his eyes, and is quiet.

Words, words, words. What a maze of "thoughts."

Sitting quietly, the roshi listens.
"Mu."
"It must be boundless, limitless."
Bell.

Why does a dog barking distract you and a bird singing does not?
I am not as calm these days as I have been.

Sitting quietly, the roshi listens.
"Mu."
"No. You have not reached the boundaries. Mu." Low, concentrated.

Yes, samadhi; that is what he wants me to experience. I have not. More effort is required. Calm, the reality sense, is one thing. Samadhi is another. A further step.

Sitting quietly, the roshi listens.
"Mu."
"You are clinging to something. You have to let go and get to nothingness. Just space and time."
Bell.

This morning before sanzen I saw that I was still striving for something. Seeing this helped with calm. Did he see the striving this morning?

This morning the roshi gave me a long, formal lecture Religion is garbed in the time, place, and nature of the people who have it. For example, Christ was persecuted, and this shows up in the religion of Christianity. In Mohammedanism stealing is not the crime that it is in Christianity, because there was a scarcity of food in early Mohammedan countries. This is an example of an environmental influence on religion.

I would like you to be clear about this point first. I would like you to get it into your head and keep it there.

Next point. The times before the Buddha resembled those before Luther. The Brahmins were in power and were unscrupulous.

The fundamental teaching of Buddhism is emancipation. The question is, how to get it. Christians have become enslaved by the idea of God. The Buddha studied with all the Brahmin sages and hermits to find out. He failed. So he wiped out the past and started zazen. This he practiced from the ages of twenty-five to thirty-one years according to historians; from the ages of twenty to thirty-one according to religious authorities. At any rate, it was for a long time. He washed away the past, all other methods. He literally bathed in a river and accepted milk from a maid, whereupon his retainers left him. He gave up all other methods, such as standing on nails and whatnot.

Zazen has some connection with Yoga techniques, but otherwise Buddhism has not. The Buddha sat under the tree for six years. He sat in the triangle (lotus) position, abandoning others. Recent excavations show that the zazen position is very ancient and predates Yoga practices. However, you can check the historical data for yourself. I am not interested in the question whether zazen is a Yoga practice. The important point is that the Buddha did zazen.

Now, what is the aim of sitting? Emancipation. From what? From the desires for: excessive honor, money, power, sexual pleasure, and sleep. Looked at differently, one sits to emancipate oneself from life, old age, sickness, and death[7]; from

184

seeking impossible things; from the fear of being separated from those whom you love. In short, the goal is to get rid of pain and suffering.

Man is in slavery. The idea is to get free. One can imagine man as being trapped in a box. Some try to get free by breaking the box. The Mahayana Buddhist method is to get free without breaking the box. This is done by looking into oneself. What is the *I*? And finding that we have to transcend the opposites—for example, that of the masculine and the feminine. Transcending the opposites is what the Buddha did for six years. Then his eyes were opened and this brought emancipation, Nirvana, which is quiet and calmness. To have the bonds on you makes no difference if you are calm.

A new point. "Zen" comes from "dyhana," which means thinking calmly, or calm thinking, or carefully weighed thinking. The things that disturb us are not outside but within. The Buddha learned this by self-reflection.

The goal is emancipation from bondage. By Zen or Zen-like training. All the Buddha's teaching came from zazen, so Zen training is zazen.

All religions must have a basic zazenlike training. Why? Because you have to have a firm starting point. Before you start to move forward you have to have a good start. And the busier a person is, the more important zazen is.

Osho, a great master, asked himself every day: "Master." He replied: "Yes, sir." "Be aware." "Yes, sir." "In the future do not be deceived by men." "Yes, sir." This was his whole teaching and training: he asked and answered himself thus.

For me Zen means only: quiet, calm, meditation.

I did not go to the United States when I was asked to because you have to teach Zen here in Japan, where you will not tell people what they want to hear and where they will see it as it is.

The Americans are a mixture, and therefore they are frank. But they have no base. Therefore Zen would be good for them.

Americans need the spiritual union of mind and body to get a basis for their culture. Zen might furnish this basis.

The East has developed spiritually because it is poor materially.

Zen has been misinterpreted to the West because those who have done the interpreting have not finished their training. So they have talked of goals instead of the method.

The Americans can transform Zen after they have learned it in Japan. But the learning must come first in Japan. (Remember that religion varies with the time, place, and people who clothe it.)

You cannot take art treasures out of their environment. They have to be seen there. Later, having seen them, you can do what you will with them in your own art.

The Japanese cannot modify Zen for the Americans, as the interpreters have tried to do. Americans have to learn it first and then modify it for themselves.

A tribe modifies religion for itself, but first it has to get religion.

The interpreters are egoists, not Buddhists. Furthermore, a man must have a feeling for humanity in order to be able to transmit a teaching. He must be like Goethe or Beethoven.

The more sincere you are, the fewer the people who will listen to you. You get on a higher level and fewer can follow. If a lot of people listen to you, you are no good.

When Osho called to himself he called himself "master," referring to the man in the box. And the "do not be deceived by men" meant "do not be deceived by money, fame, etc."

184

Next point: the first sermon of the Buddha. After six years of zazen he taught the eightfold path for getting to his enlightenment, to help ordinary people do it. (1) Correct seeing

(seeing things just as they are). (2) Right thinking. (This presupposes right seeing, for you need right ideas for right thinking. Right thinking is thinking of things as they are. We can miss doing this by, for example, under- or overestimating ourselves. So right thinking also requires a knowledge of yourself.) (3) Right speaking (expressing what you have thought correctly). (4) Right action. (5) Right effort. (Each step is based on the previous ones.) (6) Right determination (that which does not waver after the action is started). (7) Right faith. (8) Right living.

Only these eight steps are necessary for emancipation. There is no need to bow to anyone or to do anything else.

You should experience with your body, not with your head. Think with your toes, not with your head.

Why is there sanzen, you ask? By going through contradictions you come to the understanding which goes with *mu* or being nothing.[8] Also, you get to the point where you think that you understand. One who is further along knows that you do not. He discovers this in sanzen and can help you. Further, a koan is a way of enabling you to cut out your ego. Finally, it is impossible for you now to understand the use of the koan in this practice. You have to accept its use on faith. Only later would you come to understand its role.

A genius can accomplish emancipation by sitting alone. In Rinzai Zen we do it step by step. So it is often called ladder Zen.

Reflection after the lecture: despite the sound of much of this, the net effect of the lecture was to take ever more of the mystery and exoticism out of Buddhism.[9] For example, one sees from it that "seeing things as they are" = "seeing them without projecting values on them." And it comes about by being aware that we do this. That is just good psychology. Further, the general emphasis was that the goal is calmness through meditation. The high-sounding phrases in the literature of Zen Buddhism seem to be simply: (*a*) expressions of the feeling of calm (and perhaps samadhi, though I cannot speak of that), or (*b*) devices for bringing it about.

Sitting quietly, the roshi listens.
"Mu."
"That is pretty good. But penetrate."

Why was that good? Because of the way I felt: calm. And I got that way this time by seeing that just being able to stand in a store shopping with my wife and not getting frantic and not shoving in my views and not being mean is the condition of egolessness. It is as simple as that, trite and do-it-yourself as it sounds. It is not some awesome experience, transpsychic or whatever. It is just a simple everyday affair. And to think that it is something magical or that it gives magical powers is to be "ego-driven," to seek the philosopher's stone. It is just a simple, commonplace thing. The only magic about it is its rarity, and that as a result of it you behave decently (which helps others to behave decently). Of course, that is in a way magical, but not in any metaphysical sense.

No wonder they speak of the *by-products* of the "Zen" experience (feelings of oneness, sharpened perception, etc.). It is misleading to stress these, for that makes one seek the sort of effect mescaline produces, without taking it. It piles on mystery where there is no mystery.

Underlining the foregoing two paragraphs would not help. Either you want mystery or you see through it.

Sitting later, I knew that this was a step forward.

The matter-of-factness of the whole affair cannot be over-emphasized. You keep thinking it is something else, something more. It is just a man shopping with his wife without irritability. The only thing that makes it more is the enormous amount of effort necessary to achieve this simple state.

Sitting quietly, the roshi listens.
"Mu."
A quick shake of the head:
"Penetrate."
Bell.

The realization of the matter-of-factness of this work did not help today.

One can talk about Zen or from Zen. The former is relatively uninteresting. The latter requires more experience than I have had. All this, then, is simply a continuation of my work in philosophy.

Gathering information about Zen, either from books or from people, is confusing and distracting. Settling into the here and now in any circumstances is real and not confusing. Nevertheless, here is some information which helps with the latter.

(a) Going through the eight steps discussed in the lecture is a cyclical process. After reaching the last step you return to the first with greater insight and begin over again. (b) The roshi never uses the term satori. When asked about satori once, he replied that it is an experience which can accompany each major step forward, but is not important. (c) In Zen study one repeats not only the *mu* koan, but others as well. What is an answer the first time is not the second.

(d) In the 1930's, during his first three years of study, a Japanese Zen monk simply sat for the first year. He was given a koan, but he did not do sanzen. During the second year he was not required to go to sanzen every time. The third year was intensive and he was required to go every time. After that his experience was not so intense, and he might work outside the temple as well as continue his studies.

(e) Passing the first koan is crucial and requires the greatest effort. (f) It may be likened to this: There is an absolute over there beyond the phenomenal world, or so we think. The first major step is to jump over things to it. Then we gradually, in further koans, move back into the phenomenal world and see that it is the absolute. The absolute is not something beyond and behind. The so-called phenomenal world might be called manifestations of the absolute. However, there is danger of getting caught in the Zen "cave," as it is called; that is, in making the first step, liking the calm and staying there, achieving a feeling of disgust for phenomena.

The suggestion is inevitable that the process is wholly psychological.

A second long formal lecture from the roshi I want to continue my exposition and talk of the Kegon philosophy, the philosophy of Zen Buddhism. But first some preliminary remarks and a clarification of the last lecture.

I observed, during my early experience with my own teacher, that young girls of, say, twenty went ahead more rapidly with their koans than men did. My teacher explained that this was due to the fact that they had less experience than the men. However, he said that men, who have to go through more to get there than the girls do, get a firmer base in the end. And I noticed that the girls later slipped more easily.

I want to call your attention to the fact that there is no "method" in Zen study. It is solely a matter of your becoming something. At the university you were taught how to study and helped along in a positive way. In Zen study you are put on your own and the teacher leads you only by preventing you from going astray.

Descartes drew a wrong conclusion from the *Cogito:* namely, that thinking is accurate. Kant saw that thinking may err. And so in Zen study the teacher is on guard to keep the student from going astray in his thinking. The teaching is really leading you out. Indian Yogis and teachers tell you *what* you have to become.

Finally, the Zen sect is the most vital in Buddhism because its adherents stress meditation.

Now I shall examine what I said the other day from another angle, or indeed from the reverse side. In the Sermon on the Mount Christ said: "Blessed are the poor in spirit." This is what the Zen Buddhist is getting at with the teaching of no-mind. And note that Christian texts can furnish examples for Zen Buddhists. Whereas other religions say of each other that the teachings of the other are false, the Zen Buddhist can find the truth in the teachings of any religion.

Zen Buddhist philosophers have always practiced meditation. But they have also employed a certain teaching: (1) The way (tao) of the adult is to make clear his own (clear) virtue (in Zen Buddhism it is called his Buddha-nature). (2) Following this, he should help others to achieve the same condition. (3) Then in the long run all people should live peacefully. This is what the Buddhists call Nirvana.

Now, how do we achieve these three things? By five steps: (*a*) stopping all disturbances in you from the environment; (*b*) samadhi (getting fixed into motionlessness); (*c*) being quiet; (*d*) being at ease; and (*e*) examining yourself (what is this I?).

(Note that these five elements in the Kegon "how" are not so much ways of achieving peace as they are steps in the process.)

What is it that you attain by this? Quiet. You proceed by going over and over these five steps, each time getting a bit better at it. You get calm one day, and then you see that this was not calm and you make another step. You have to keep on and on and on. By training you can bring yourself to keep on developing.

The foregoing is a clarification of the last lecture. Now for the Kegon philosophy (contained in the *Kegon Sutra*).

Out of the mud can come a lotus.

Consider the Crystal Palace of Indra. In each crystal every other crystal is reflected. And that reflection is reflected. So is it with people. Each affects the other, and so on ad infinitum.

I am here because of my parents and they because of theirs. In ten generations you have so-and-so-many people involved. In thirty generations you have, I believe, a hundred million people involved. And we are still at the beginning of human life on this earth.

190 Now we have myself here, as a result of all this past, and you. All this past effort is crystallized in each of us. This is the temporal aspect.

Now for the spatial. I eat rice which is grown by this man, wear clothes made by those men, and so on. It is estimated that one hundred thousand people are involved in keeping me going *now*. You may say: "I went to Osaka by train"—but think of the people involved in producing that train and making that journey possible!

So the Zen attitude is to bow in all directions to give thanks to all. And if you understand this gratitude you try to serve society. This is the life of what we call the Bodhisattva, the man who understands.

191 The way of the adult is to bow in all directions. Then you are living according to the great teaching. A Bodhisattva takes a vow to devote himself to society for all his lives.

So you have Manju, Fugen, and Kwannon, the central Bodhisattvas (of intuitive wisdom, harmony, and kindness) in the Zen philosophy. Of these Fugen is the chief one.

If you understand the thanks you owe to all, you give your

life to service. But this must not be confused with pantheism, for you are not worshiping a spirit in things. Mainly, however, it must not be confused with pantheism, because that confusion leads Westerners to think that Buddhism is idolatry.

Sitting quietly, the roshi listens.
"Mu."
"You have understood this pretty well. But you still have not made it. You still have a little way to go. When you go home to your position the day after tomorrow, I want you to continue with zazen, with meditation. Nothing is energy. You should see that. Nothing is energy."[10]
Bell.

Sitting quietly, the roshi listens.
"Mu."
"Keep going as you are. Penetrate further through all space and time. Like this." He looks down and gives a low "Mu."

It is as though he were trying to show me the condition of no-mind, and this suggests that if I just kept on doing my "mu" as he does it, it would eventually come right.

"Going through or beyond space and time," as I have seen before, can mean: getting into the here and now. It can also mean: getting beyond the ideas of space and time. And these come to the same thing. For strictly speaking, in a way there are no space and time, for (*a*) "space" and "time" are just instruments; (*b*) "space" and "time" are just names, and if you do not use them you cannot speak of space and time (a tautology); and (*c*) in the here and now there are no space and time.

It is well to bear especially (*a*) in mind when you speak of the thing-*mu*. Indeed, if you bear it in mind for all that you can

193

say in philosophy, you get a real feeling for egolessness and "there are no substances."

I now feel far beyond "Philosophical Reflections."

The talk could go on and on. It should not. And yet for a while it must. For I can say "mu" now, but I am not far along. I imagine that eventually I will say only "mu." Then I will talk again. As a man, never as a philosopher. The philosopher says only: "Mu." After he has done philosophy: *mu*.

NOTES

1. The resemblance of the procedures and atmosphere to those of a military camp is inescapable, although the training is to such a completely different end.

2. The roshi had been a philosophy student before he took his Zen training.

3. See the writer's "Wittgenstein and the Naming Relation," *Inquiry,* Vol. 7, No. 4 (1964).

4. One must bear in mind that the calm spoken of here is not that of apathy.

5. Eugene Herrigel, *Zen in the Art of Archery* (New York: Pantheon Bks. Inc., 1953).

6. See p. 164.

7. In response to a question, he said that it is the *ideas* of these things we are trying to be rid of.

8. He pointed out in another connection that contradictions are built into us by living, giving as an example: a child wants so-and-so, and his father says that he cannot have it.

9. Part of this impression was due to the roshi's behavior during the lecture, and to things that happened during the lecture at which only I and an interpreter were present. (The roshi did not feel that his English was good enough for a lecture, although it sufficed for

sanzen.) On the one hand, the roshi was extremely businesslike and matter of fact. There was no suggestion in his manner of delivery of a priest talking. On the other hand, there was a pause for a "coffee break" (tea), and another for him to change his kimono, which became drenched with perspiration from the efforts he was making. One could not feel that he was talking about anything exotic or esoteric. Both what he said and the manner in which he said it indicated that he was being thoroughly practical about life.

10. The roshi had been given a paper of mine called "Philosophy and Nothing" (*Chicago Review* [Summer, 1959]). An advanced student of his told me that the roshi had said to him: "Wienpahl writes about nothing, but he does not understand it. I have got to make him understand." Otherwise I suppose that he might have used "mu" in the foregoing. See also "Philosophical Reflections" in the same issue of the *Chicago Review*. These reflections led me to go to Japan.

CHAPTER EIGHT

NOW GO IN AND LOOK AGAIN. RETURN AND REPEAT THE STEPS WITH what is now known.[1]

1, 43: Note how I assumed it was: You have to understand the "mu," and not: you have to understand *mu*.

2, 43: I was to learn later that it takes a long time to get rid of the "thoughts" entirely. However, becoming aware of them and noting them helps in controlling them. Being completely rid of them may be a description of samadhi.

3, 46: "Can Joshu's answer be an expression of his Buddha-nature?" What a question now! Of course "mu" is.

4, 47: Of course, look at the roshi. He shows the answer as he sits quietly and says: "Mu."

5, 47: "Listening" is like using a language: it follows *learning to use it*. One cannot merely "listen" to the koan. One must struggle and learn its use. Then one verily *is mu*. Thus the openness and "passivity" are results, not instinctive things. They are the "ignorance" which comes from "knowledge"— as spontaneous language comes from learning it the hard way.

6, 48: You and it are one when it is solved: no dualism.

7, 48: The "mu" helps to do this in two ways: this, and by just saying nothing but "mu" to yourself during zazen.

8, 48: Since this account is chronological, early "definitive" statements are not definitive.

9, 49: It is worth noting that I later give a bark as an answer; that is, get back to the record and away from the question. So does the intellect (the logic of words) outstrip us.

10, 51: The subtlety of the *mu* koan is glimpsed here: I have not only to give the sort of answer which Joshu gave, I have to give that answer; and it is the core of the "philosophy" of Buddhism: the "doctrines" of egolessness, of no-mind, of non-duality, of samadhi.

11, 51: To show what "mu" means is to be *mu*.

12, 51: The answer has to come from you because you have to be *mu* (nothing, egoless, aware that there is no self). What I was getting at on p. 000 is not bad. However, I did not know it then. I was still treating the koan as a puzzle. ——The stuff is good because the answers to koans are nonsense, for they are not in words, although they are often given by means of words. ——By p. 00 it is evident that I was beginning to *use* some of the things I had read in the literature of Zen Buddhism.

However, it is well to bear in mind that this report and the process of which it is an account are chronological. This raises the question: how definitive are the immediately foregoing "definitive" statements? How can I sound off about koans when I have not even passed one koan?

13, 51: Notice the confusion of word and thing here, "mu" and *mu,* verbal answer and what it means; and, *hence,* the dualism here, for confusion can only occur where we think that there is separateness, when, that is in this case, we cannot *use* a word. ——This also shows how saying that there are such confusions does not prevent their occurrence.

14, 52: Notice how confused this painting simile was and how it got in the way. The answer is not from you, it *is* you.

15, 52: But compare it also to: Does the dog have Buddha-nature? No!

16, 52: Yes, beyond *mental* acts or the *idea that* there are mental acts. However, Zen is getting beyond the concepts as words too. Yet getting beyond the notion that there are mental acts is a small form of overcoming dualism.

17, 52: Yes, just live your everyday life, be practical.

197

18, 52: Notice the doubts which go with not having the answer, beautiful as this one seemed. ——Only later did I realize that answers to koans are logical. I was still misled here by a preconception, gained from reading, that they are not logical.

19, 52: What was involved here is clearer now: I had stayed in the world of my existence, that is, in philosophy, to give this answer. You have to go beyond your own particular "world" as well as beyond the world.

20, 53: "Go logically" = "I can use these words now" = "I understand these words." ——On the other hand, I say, "I can use the words." I should say, "I have *a* use for the words" not *the* use. This is the trap and wonder of conceptual, logical relations. They do enable one to move from fact to fact while evading the facts themselves. And then if one knows how to use them, one can get back to original use.

21, 53: All the metaphors in here (art, child-conception, etc.) are of things external to oneself. They are alien seeds which grow *in* one and then are expelled as independent entities. ——All traps, for the outcome is better spoken of as becoming one with the koan and *mu*.

22, 54: Notice the dualism in here and the questions about it.

23, 54: Think of learning to use a term and contrast that with using it. Thinking resolves doubts; philosophic thinking, philosophic doubts.

24, 55: How deep the puzzlements go (to use this language); even after you get through intellectualism intellectually, you have a long way to go.

25, 55: The "we" here should very likely be "I."

26, 56: The mystic is he who lives practically, automatically, with thought intervening only when there is a practical problem. Yet he also lives with awareness. ——However, "impractical" thought, philosophic thought, may have to occur to bring about this stage.

27, 57: *Under* all this verbiage lies the answer.

28, 58: "Transcend existence and nonexistence" is not the meaning of "mu." It is a way to get to its meaning.

29, 58: Don't interpret; that is, respond without letting thought get in the way, that is, words, although the response may be verbal.

30, 58: If you responded this way, you would be *mu* (egoless).

31, 58: There is a connection here with Wittgenstein's work. If you just spit out the answer you would be responding automatically. When you can do that, when you are *mu,* then you might answer differently if he gave you the *mu* koan again later. For then there would be an interchange between two enlightened (egoless) people. This shows the answer to: how can there be more than one answer to a koan, given the claim (true) that each koan has *a* classical answer? It is: after many steps have been taken, the whole matter is quite otherwise. Egolessness, so to speak, puts a different light on it.

That "egoless" can follow "enlightenment" in parentheses (above) indicates that egolessness comes with getting free of the *idea* of a self.

32, 58: It takes two to play the game. This is one of the reasons for saying that the "mind" or zen can only be transmitted from person to person. (See *The Zen Teaching of Huang Po.*[2]) Another reason: it cannot be transmitted in words or by books because it is a nonverbal thing.

33, 60: One satori, or better step (remember the *by*-products), gets you to the other shore? Certainly, but then comes the next step, and the next. Remember Hakuin's innumerable small satoris and seven great ones.

34, 63: "Body and mind merge, too . . ." That is, when the illusions are under control. Merging the mind and the body is a psychological process, for they are separate only in thought.

35, 63: "You have to get beyond existence down there."

"Beyond existence" down there? No, what it means. You have got to get beyond existence down there.

36, 63: No, they do not mean: beyond the *ideas* of existence, etc. They mean just what they say. However, there is something to be said for the observation on p. 63, for in fact both ways of putting the matter come to the same thing. Is this confusing word and thing? Is not overcoming dualism doing just that or something like it? Here is where the distinction between word and thing may mislead, and the use of quotation marks in recent logic. This would not obviate the importance of: A rose by any other name would smell as sweet.

37, 64: Either language is all right provided that you do not interpret one on the basis of the other. That is, each works in its own context, but does not work in the context of the other, which is what people find when they try it, and is the reason why they say it's nonsense to believe in reincarnation.

38, 66: In view of all this interpreting, in what sense of the term "know" could it be said that I then knew what "mu" meant? The knowledge was still intellectual. It was all still words and clarification of language. I saw where the terms led but I was not there yet. This is like at last seeing a destination from a vantage point, seeing it from far away, but having no sense yet of how to get there. Thus at the next sanzen I said that the *mu* is I, and the roshi properly asked: "And what is I?"

39, 67: Compare my response to the question, "Was ist das Ich?" at that time with a subsequent response (see pp. 163, 164).

40, 69: Could this feeling of happiness be the beginning of the awareness of calm?

41, 69: Notice what happened during sesshin, when there was no speaking or reading or writing going on.

42, 70: Having a blank mind is in a way having the answer. It is a step further just to say "mu."

43, 76: Compare "lose yourself" with "lose the *idea* of yourself." At first the latter seems better. However, in fact the two phrases seem to come to the same thing, and thus to indicate that the distinction between the material and the formal modes of speech may be misleading.[3]

44, 77: This seems like Spinoza in modern garb. For the "metaphysical" portion (corresponding to Part I in the *Ethics*), you have "no metaphysics" instead of "a consistent monism." For the rest, it is the working out of the consequences of "no metaphysics" for living; that is, for ethics. Otherwise the new twist is the sitting (meditation) both in fact and in the talk about the matter (both in fact and in "theory"). ——Think too of Sartre's description of his work as a working out of the assumption that God does not exist.

Theoretically speaking, Spinoza solved the problem of dualism, overcame dualism. One can only wonder that one still hears about the mind-body problem; indeed, that one is oneself somehow subtly involved in it.

45, 78: Note Locke's *tabula rasa,* the Zen Buddhists' *no-mind,* and the roshi's interest in political democracy. The interest lies, not in the nature of the first two in themselves, but in the similar results of using these conceptions.

46, 79: And yet that was just the thing to do: concentrate on "mu." Mu, mu, mu. To break the language spell.

47, 79: (*b*) shows how far I was from the answer.

48, 79: Back to logic.

49, 79: It now seems that it is not reasoning at all.

50, 80: "Inferred" from: Every true proposition is analytic. So too did Spinoza get his view from seeing that there can be only one substance (i. e., no *substances*), apparently by carrying the subject-predicate logic to its extreme. ——These seemingly completely abstract theoretical considerations have practical bearings.

51, 80: It sometimes seems that all philosophers see this by whatever route they travel. Think of Hume on liberty and necessity. It is just a matter of coming to accept things as they are. And they are not consistent. Only logic is consistent. The battle then is: not to be trapped by logic, hence by the intellect. The intellect is fine, just do not get trapped by it; by words, that is.

52, 80: The koan will speak with words; but it is what the words say that counts, not the words.

53, 83: That was it.

54, 83: Instead of *make* it work, let it work.

55, 83: This sort of thing shows how far I was from the simple answer: "mu."

56, 85: This natural leading into values from facts was noted again and again and in various ways, but often with the feeling that it would be quite hard to make clear to others that the one follows from the other. For another example, as a result of concentrating one gets strong, and in strength lies decent behavior, for then one is not ambitious nor does one dissipate (to dissipate is to dissipate one's energies, and that goes with the dissolute life).

With the later realization of one's identity with the world and therefore with other people, I saw more clearly how one can speak of natural as opposed to conventional morality. (See p. 163, together with comments on that page. See also p. 119 on the ancestors). Philosophers like Dewey have said that man is naturally neither good nor evil. He becomes good or evil according to his environment. I think it may be added that the enlightened (free, self-aware) man is naturally good, and thus *in a sense* men are naturally good.

57, 89: This shows how it is something in us, the ideas we have, that misleads.

58, 89: This question can be given a simple answer. Or rather, the answer to it *is* simple. The difficulty lies in seeing it: that is, it lies in us. (See also Chap. Three, n. 8, and p. 155, together with comment 158 thereon).

59, 89: Always *showing* reality—a variation of talking about it instead of being it. The dualism still remains in its radical form though exorcised in a special form.

60, 89: Always trying to give an answer (word) led to missing the meaning of that word, the thing. Of course the answer to the koan is not verbal, if you mean by "answer" what the answer *means* (if you mean by "answer" what "answer" means).

61, 90: It appears here that I had to get in touch with reality, that is, break away from the Joshu story, and *then* afterward begin to see how "mu" expresses the reality at which I was already pointing.

62, 90: *Mu* or "mu"?

63, 90: This seems to make it "mu" and not *mu*.

64, 90: I had it here and did not know it.

65, 91: This shows how one can get to the meaning of a word without knowing it; that is, use it without knowing that one is, for I was not then trying consciously to become *mu*.

66, 91: One seems inevitably to want the answer and to want the whole thing to be purely verbal.

67, 91: "When the word and the things are one" = "when the word is used" = "when the word is transparent." It is hard to see this, because it is often important (for other purposes) to distinguish the word from the thing (for example, in learning to use the word).

68, 92: How can I and the word "mu" be one? This should read: "when I am *mu*," not "when I am 'mu'".

69, 92: The superhuman task of teaching philosophy (life) by books.

70, 92: Was the later stopping of sanzen a resistance to becoming *mu*,—that and the idea that I had a soul? Possibly, but they were also on the way to accepting sanzen (instead of having to take it) and to getting through that idea.

71, 93: To be your answer is to stand under it, to understand it.

72, 94: What makes a question meaningless? Our interpretation of it, our attitude toward it. So meaningless questions can be used to break out of interpreting (thinking). (See comment 58, p. 202.)

73, 94: What does that "it" refer to? Apparently to "mu." It should refer to *mu*. When to put quotes around "mu" finally became confusing. Then the confusion cleared.

74, 95: It *is* Joshu's answer!

75, 96: Becoming the answer = becoming what the word means, not the word.

76, 100: All this is a technique for achieving tranquillity and not to be taken literally *by Westerners until* we have learned this language.

77, 100: This shows that I still did not *know* that "mu" is the answer.

This day's work (pp. 96–100) brings out the steplike character of zen study. I had made a step and was relaxing.

78, 102: Notice that the "Woof" answer fits the anecdote about Joshu and the monk but not the *koan,* which is: What did the "mu" mean? On the other hand, Joshu's answer in the anecdote is the answer to the koan.

79, 102: Allowing for spontaneity overlooks the steps forward that are taken, by means of which one comes to accept discipline and see that one can be bound by "spontaneity" as well as by "discipline."

80, 106: This helps to make clear how there might be other answers to the koan in subsequent work on it when one comes back to it later; answers such as "Woof." (See above comment 31, p. 199.)

81, 109: It involves the whole individual if you really believe, for example, that there are no philosophic problems.

82, 109: Of course, you could call "making it have to do with the life of a man" religion. If you do, then what I am doing is not philosophy. It is good, therefore, that I am seeing through Zen Buddhism too.

83, 109: It is the soul or self problem. Does a man have a soul? Therefore it is connected with the meaning problem (if you think you have a soul you look for the meaning of life), and with the death problem (if you think that you are a self, you fear death), and with the problem of evil (if you think you have a soul you believe in good and evil—see p. 163, together with comment 160). It is apparently well said that the *mu* koan is the greatest and deepest of koans.

84, 110: The notion that there is no substance to be called "mind" is both right and completely wrong. There is this sort of "experience of the mind" (hence the notion is wrong), and there is the substance-attribute metaphysics (hence the notion is right). This shows how unempirical we can be. That morning I had direct experiences in the light of which I saw clearly that it is all right to use the term mind as a substantive for some purposes. In other contexts it is misleading to do so.

85, 110: Just zazen (any *practice*). How right. Doing it until the quiet of it pervades all of your activities. There is no intellectual problem except the one we create.

86, 110: It is one thing to think of a word, another to use it. Thinking of no-mind is being dualistic. Having it is having overcome dualism.

87, 112: It is getting beyond words; words extend us into the past and future. ——One can object to this that it is trite. That shows that the doing is hard, the knowing simple.

88, 115: "Direct vs. mediated knowledge" is related to "know (carnal knowledge) vs. know (science)," and both "direct knowledge" and "carnal knowledge" make "know thyself" clearer, more useful.

89, 115: Notice in through here how much the question of what a *word* is is involved.

90, 115. There is no answer and there is an answer. Only this is not paradoxical. It is logical. What makes a question meaningless is that we want more of an answer than is the proper answer. We complicate what is simple. So there is no answer to the complication, but there is to the simple part of the question.

91, 117: That is, when you are *mu,* egoless, you can avoid getting caught up in a verbal interchange. You can accept it or reject it (this also shows that being egoless is a matter of strength, not passivity). What is a meaningless question? One in which you get stuck, one that involves you. If you are egoless you do not get stuck in a question. You can accept an answer.

92, 117: You really believe that the riddle does not exist by being egoless, when you are egoless.

93, 117: No, you do not say: "The 'mu' means *mu.*" That *is* just logic. You just say: "Mu."

94, 120: It is not only language that traps us, in the use of which Platonism lurks. It is feelings and emotions too.

95, 120: You do not get rid of the ego. You control it, and this by being aware of it. So the process is "intellectual." ——One says "by being aware of it." It would be less misleading to say: "by being aware of this thought, that feeling, etc., which make 'it' up." For there is no ego, and to speak of it is just a way of talking.

To think that philosophy is more than this is to make it impractical, theoretical. That is Platonism too, and one of the thoughts that ensnare.

96, 121: The limit of Western thought: to stop thinking and

doing what we know we should. Thinking often reinforces dualism.

97, 122: And "it" is in you, as you find when you get below all ideas, including that of the self. Now just go ahead and do it. *Mu*.

98, 124: As though he cannot see me!

99, 124: And, since you and the world are one, this is why Sakyamuni held up the flower instead of lecturing when asked once to expound his teaching. ——However, the disciple who "got" the teaching and smiled, just smiled. He did not say anything.

100, 124: This account cannot be logical and atemporal. It is and can only be a report. The solution of the mind-body problem lies in its dissolution, and of this one can only report. Intellectual solutions to the problems have already been given.

101, 124: Notice how it is all already there. After this I "should" have just sat.

102, 125: Later I learned that the roshi simply used this form of idealism to get an image in my mind which, in turn, I could use in developing concentration. For later he said that a Zen Buddhist can use, and does use where appropriate, a text from *any* philosophy to bring about the result at which he is aiming. There is no Zen philosophy, that is, except in that there is the report that there is none.

103, 125: It is not a theory. It is a device for producing an effect, or for expressing that effect.

104, 126: The quest was still there, sensed then but standing out like a sore thumb now. Being on the other shore = seeing that the quest is still there. Notice how easy it is to shift back to the puzzle angle, the intellectual aspect.

105, 127: Aha! "There is only logical necessity" is not an ontological truth. It is a device for taking a step, or a report on such a step. I have been making it into an ontological truth. Of course the body *has* to behave in these and these ways, *when* the matter is looked at in a certain way.

106, 127: The doctrine makes sense, but only if it be assumed that there is an I—which I was doing here.

107, 127: A way of describing being free: seeing that only practical problems exist.

108, 127: "Heady instead of solid" is appropriate here, for I had just come across another idea. Nevertheless, a step was made.

The further step of getting into the position in which one can take or leave the koan study is approaching. It seems that, unless one has made such a step, one can scarcely appreciate it.

109, 129: Notice that I was aware of the ambiguity of "answer" as it comes to be used in zen study, yet it continued to plague me. (It refers to an answer to the koan and to the state brought about by koan study.)

110, 130: Here again is an approach to morality which is not conventional. The self-aware man is naturally good—not good for some purpose, such as self-preservation.

111, 130: Despite these remarks about (*a*) I fell into the trap of thinking that there really are an I and an ego.

112, 132: I was not only in contact with the *idea* of the self at this time, as the caution about the metaphor shows. There was also the experience itself. The last two sentences of this paragraph apply to the experience as well as to the "self."

113, 134: I knew what the state should be though I was not in it. Hence: (*a*) know the answer: "mu"; (*b*) know the answer: be *mu*; and (*c*) know the answer: know that being *mu* is the "answer."

I was aware of the ambiguity of "answer" as it comes to be used in zen study, yet the ambiguity continued to be bothersome. It is worthwhile to compare the foregoing sentence with comment 109, p. 208. Which plagued me, the "answer" or its ambiguity? Can one not say: "The word plagues me because of its ambiguity?" The *word* plagues me. One might be inclined to think that the second "it" in comment 109 should be replaced by "the ambiguity." On the other hand, the ambiguity of a word is the meaning of a word. An ambiguous word has two meanings. That the second "it" in comment 109 can refer either to "ambiguity" or to "answer" shows how a word *is* its meaning. The third "it" in comment 109 is thus all right. It refers to "answer" by referring to the second "it." It does not need to be replaced by "the word." When words are used one does not think of their meanings. It is then that they *are* their meanings.

114, 134: An interesting facet of the *mu* koan: the question, though meaningless, has its "answer" in it: "mu"; and that answer refers to the state of egolessness.

115, 135: Since we now know that there is no self (that to speak of one is a manner of speaking), this might be put: Why should a living creature strive to live? It just lives. Reality just is. Striving is a psychological affair. ——Looked at from another angle, of course striving, too, is a part of reality.

116, 135: How simple it seems now to do all this by just saying "Mu!"

117, 135: I now think that the "not yet" meant that I had not had samadhi, which is defined as the condition of profound concentration in which the mind identifies with itself. Zen teachers talk matter-of-factly about this condition and urge students to strive for it. I do not know whether it is the same as having the mind "drop down." For my purposes the answers to such questions are unimportant.

118, 135: The Zen idealist "philosophy" is a consequence of the egoless doctrine.

119, 136: How curiously the fact of being bothered by death can come out as not liking the internality of relations theory.

120, 136: Essences are words. This paragraph suggests that so-called philosophical theories can lead to experiences if their "advice" is taken. The "no concepts" thing leads to tranquillity. A "consequence" of instrumentalism is tranquillity.

121, 136: The thought of an answer gets in the way of an answer.

122, 136: In a sense what one does with the *mu* koan is to learn to listen to the *Sinn* of the koan. As for the other koans I cannot say. On the other hand, "mu" means egolessness and so the answer to the koan fits with *interpretations* of the answer. This koan is amazingly compact.

123, 137: Why, then, did I not start as of then saying "Mu" at every sanzen? (*a*) I did not know how to say that I was ego-less, and (*b*) I had not listened to the koan (to the *Sinn*) in which the way is given: by saying "Mu" (not intending to, so to speak—just saying it). ——Also I had not attained any degree of egolessness.

Those who say that one answer does for all the koans are concerned with the *Bedeutung* and not with the *Sinn;* or, as might now be said, with the meaning and not the use of the koans.

124, 137: Another way of looking at nonduality—when a word is used transparently, when (to put it oddly) it is its meaning, or when it and its meaning are not separated. Seen this way, words are ghostly affairs. No wonder that they have caused us to think of a separate and subsistent realm. "Actually" they are just as physical as anything. This shows, too, that the job is a psychological one; in a sense it is a matter of the way we take words. The goal is not to be aware of them.

125, 137: The task in contemporary philosophy: standing under what we know. It takes not only work but self-awareness. That is why philosophy in the work of Wittgenstein and Heidegger, for example, has turned back on itself. This turning back on itself is a sign, or a part, of the turning back on the self of the individual. A step in philosophy: instrumentalism. The next step: self-consciousness. The next step: no philosophy. (Yet each new generation and person will do it, for one can only free oneself.)

And that is why it is so important to emphasize sitting now. Talking may help, of course, but the sitting comes first.

126, 138: These practices surprised me, as had the squabbles in the history of the psychoanalytic movement. How can "enlightened" people quarrel with each other? I finally realized that this disillusionment resulted from an idea I had of which I was unaware: the idea that people can be *completely* reasonable. I eventually saw that even the most enlightened man is still an animal, that is, still human.

127, 138: The notion of satori was still bothersome then. It helped to see that satori is a by-product, and not a necessary one, of innumerable small steps toward the state of calm. Each step is in its way sudden, but the notion of sudden complete enlightenment is misleading.

128, 139: Different ways of life, different garbs for the same thing.

129, 139: The ego talking? It could have been the I, or both.

130, 139: This simply explains a facet of the notion of sudden enlightenment. Actually the process is a lengthy and continuing one which consists of many steps. Coming to know directly that you have an ego is one. At the time it occurs it may seem like a huge step, and therefore the final one. Hence, "sudden" enlightenment. As remarked above, in a way all the steps are sudden.

131, 139: Yes, sanzen can be a crutch. It can also be a device for getting rid of crutches. Nothing wrong with sanzen. The trouble is always in you.

132, 139: There is one of the answers to those who believe

that mysticism can be chemically induced. It also clears up mysticism a bit. Having visions is not mysticism, though it may be a by-product of work toward mysticism. Mysticism is being able to see a garden for what it is. Drugs may help one to do that? Possibly. But mysticism also requires training and self-discipline and strength. It is a common-sense, hardheaded everyday condition, though uncommon because it requires work. It is you being in touch with the realities. It is not an exotic psychic state.

133, 139: Acting on your own is going along with circumstances, behaving automatically, although with a full awareness of the circumstances. It is nonego behavior, which the act of quitting sanzen was not, although it was a step toward such behavior (a step connected with the fact that doubt and puzzlement "lead," or may lead, to clarity).

134, 140: That union occurs when thinking is to the point, when the engine is not idling; when, so to speak, you are *not* thinking.

135, 140: Yes, and when I can *do* it whenever I want to—

136, 141: Still not seeing that quiet *is* it, enlightenment. Looking at it as a method. Hence, still thinking of a goal. One can be quiet in anything he does. But of course there are degrees of quiet, and each step into it leads to another. Too, there is quiet and quiet: that of life and that of death and that of zen study, which is also strength and concentration.

On the other hand, one can get trapped by "goal" and come to believe that you cannot speak of zen study in terms of goals. Take a step and you find that you can. It is a reasonable way of speaking, provided one is not misled by it.

137, 141: So evident now that this was just another step.

138, 141: *"Want"* is right. "Want" means: I lack it. It also means: I desire it.

139, 141: See how close the two meanings of *real* can become: "existential" and "important," the factual and the valuational uses.

140, 142: This paragraph might be taken as a theory about human nature. It might also be taken as a description of how I felt after the step was taken.

141, 143: Here again are seeds of the notion that there is a natural morality as well as conventional moralities. I felt this more and more as the work continued. The notion has it, almost, that a man is born good and that this goodness comes out when his self (to use that language) comes out; that is, when he is enlightened. Perhaps it is better to say that it is not that a man is naturally good, but that an enlightened man is naturally good.

142, 143: It was, of course, just a step. The notion that one solves a koan is misleading. One does, but to emphasize this is to obscure the fact that the process is one of making steps forward in the development of calm.

143, 143: Needed? Who needed it? Could not be the self; it has no needs. The process? By the way, whether or not the talk of the self gives you the willies, it fitted the situation then. Realizing that, too, helps to understand the talk of the free-willers. It makes sense. Just don't become wedded to it.

144, 143: I had thought that the structure of a language determines the way a people think. A philologist denied this, although he could see the uncomfortable conclusion to which this leads: namely, that thoughts are ghostly things for which words are the names. What to do about this? It is not that the language structure has important influences on the way people think—although fixed ideas about a certain structure may have influences. It is that *language* does; or rather, loosely, that language behavior is one kind of thinking and that it (whatever the language structure) leads to dualism, to getting involved with concepts and intellectualism. Just using language has, or can have, this result. It leads to the dualism of word and thing.

This misleads when, on certain occasions, it is overlooked and one gets caught in language. Hence, it becomes important to stress the use of a word rather than its meaning on these occasions, to bring language back to working.

145, 145: This is important in the matter of what "answer" means when it is used with "koan."

146, 145: This makes it clear that zen study is not an intellectual thing in the ordinary sense of that term. Notice, too, how clear it should have been then that the answer to the koan is "mu" and yet how I continued to fumble. "They have eyes but they do not see."

147, 146: Still under the illusion that there is *one* step or a final goal. There is no one philosophic problem. ——Here one may see too, in connection with comment 136, p. 212, that it is all right to speak of *goals*. It is talk of *the* goal that is misleading. Goals but not a goal.

148, 146: This may now be seen to be most important. *The* discovery (which brings peace) is that you do not *have* to do philosophy. I had thought it meant that you *will* not thereafter. Why did Wittgenstein come back to philosophy? One does because the discovery is just another step. You go on to do philosophy, but at a deeper level; and you can leave off when other things are more important. One can be caught in a trap doing philosophy and one can be caught in a trap of not doing it (i. e., when you have to do either). Hence, the importance of the "free act": after it you are doing philosophy on your own, before it you are not. To put this in another way: before it you do not know why you are doing philosophy, after it you do. ——Certainly things look different "on the other shore." You find yourself accepting what you have been rejecting, and less likely to reject.

149, 147: The resolution of the so-called paradoxes in Zen: making one of these steps. Because of a change in you you can do two things which looked contradictory but are not.

Characteristics of these steps: (*a*) they might be called steps toward freedom, (*b*) they are often exciting, (*c*) they open up new vistas, (*d*) they resolve a paradox, (*e*) after each step connections may be seen where none were apparent before, and (*f*) they may be accompanied by satori. (The term "satori" may be used by others to refer to what is here called a step. In that event, satori in [*f*] refers to an experience of identity with something, anything whatever.)

150, 147: Now it seems better to say: solved a characteristic philosophic problem. For it now seems that there are problems with a special mark: they are paradoxes. However, it is something to have experienced the type. To say that there are *problems* is to say that there are *steps*. The notion of sudden enlightenment implies that there is *a* step.

151, 147: Even after this, other interpretations loomed. At this point the seeing that "mu" means *mu* was a kind of logical "seeing," an inference. Only later did the direct experience of the "mu" in the koan come with a moment of complete "listening."

152, 150: One can see now how, for want of a better word, one would speak of the mind. Physical things are diffuse and not just in the here and now. (They are never small enough.) A term which has no temporal and spatial reference is better, that is the point. For the here and now is neither spatial nor temporal.

It seems now that the fact that the process is one of *steps* (plural) cannot be overemphasized, even though the notion implies something to which the steps are directed and is thus misleading. Once a step is made things, look different; everything changes except, finally, the realization that a further step will eventually be made.

153, 150: "To be in the here and now" is not an interpretation of "pure mind." It gives the meaning of it. Notice how words mean other words. This is another way of seeing why one should look for the use and not for the meaning. It brings words and things back together. Looking for the meaning keeps them separate and leaves one in the realm of words—a form of the idealist frame of mind.

154, 151: It is apparent now that the language of the self and the ego which accompanied this step was part of the binding action which the step had.

155, 152: It is also wrong because, at a further stage, one sees that there is no inner and no outer, and hence no need for two languages. Thinking that there is an inner and an outer is a step to seeing that there is neither. Hence, it is also right to say that there is no language of the inner.

156, 153: Definition of "being a self": "doing zazen." Marks of "being a self": rigor, simplicity, austerity, neutrality.

157, 155: I did not realize then how important this remark was. I was still thinking of somehow solving a koan and was not sufficiently aware of the koan's relation to meditation; at least of the *mu* koan's relation to this. The answer to that koan is relatively simple. Work on the koan mainly consists in using "mu" to become *mu*.

158, 155. The whole question of the nature and role of meaningless questions now strikes me as enormously complicated. For example, there seems to be a respect in which they have simple and direct answers in the way meaningful questions do; at least, those of them do which have been called philosophical questions or puzzlements. What makes these meaningless when seen in this light is the fact that we neither see nor can accept those answers because we somehow interfere with the process of seeing the answer to a given question. We interpret and project and get caught up in chains of reasoning. For example, what does "mu" mean? *Mu*. But the temptation to interpret and get away from the answer is almost inescapable. Another example: does the external world exist? Sure. (It is worth rereading Chapter One in this light.) Another example: what is reality? In one way there seems to be no answer. Considering the matter as we are now, the answer is simple: look at it. (See the foregoing comments in this chapter: 24, p. 198; 31, 199; 58, p. 202; 72, p. 204; 80, p. 204; 83, p. 205; 90, p. 206; 91, p. 206; 104, p. 207; 114, p. 209; 120, p. 210; 115, p. 215; 171, p. 222; 185, p. 224. See also Chap. Two, note 7.)

159, 158: This is a good example of interpretation vs. listening. I interpreted what he said ("as though to say—"). What the roshi *did* was to give the answer. Only listening was necessary.

160, 163: Here again are seeds of natural morality. We *are* reality. Therefore, looked at in one way we are all one. Thus my behavior toward you is behavior toward myself.[4] If I hurt you I hurt myself. If I help you I help myself. Putting it this way, however, brings out a queer twist in the matter. For, since you and I are one, it makes no sense to speak of my good behavior toward you as altruistic. What we customarily think of as good and evil go by the board. "Good" and "evil" turn out to be manners of speaking which go with thinking that you and I and all people are separate beings.

Now, I said above that *looked at in one way* we are all one. I had to say this because, looked at in another way, we are clearly all of us separate beings. There are, *so to speak,* the absolute world and the relative world. But the point is that these two worlds do not differ, they are not separate worlds, they are the same world. It is only that we think they are different, and then, perhaps, that one or the other of them does not exist. However, we *do* think they are different worlds. And this is all right, because thinking is thinking for some purpose. One can accept this as one begins even to glimpse and only slightly experience "thinking" to no purpose, no-mind, calm, strength. After just a few steps have been taken there is seen to be no paradox, no contradiction in the statement that the relative world (the world of separate beings) is the absolute world (the world in which everything is one).

Nonsense, you will say. To which the answer is: be empirical. Make the experiment. Look and see. As Wittgenstein said: don't think, look.

(For other seeds of natural morality see comments: 17, p. 196; 44, p. 77; 56, p. 202; 110, p. 208; 141, p. 213; 191, p. 225.)

161, 164: I wish now, for whatever it is worth, to emphasize the extraordinary character of this experience; mainly to stress its matter-of-fact quality, for even in this brief description it sounds exotic. It was not. It seemed quite natural. It *was* quite natural.

I did not see until months later that the roshi had given me another koan that day: Was ist das Ich? Why I had not seen this before I do not know. Possibly because I went right back from the new koan to the *mu* koan. The impression at the time that this was that old metaphysics stuff helps to make this clear. ——And the new koan was solved immediately, as the emotions associated with this experience indicate. I mention this despite the implications some people will draw from it, because I think that it may help to put koan study in a more realistic perspective. Koans are sometimes, as I now see it, difficult; sometimes easy. A koan can be used to further work on another koan. Once again, it is not the answer to the koan that counts. It is the work. It is not the goal; it is the process that counts. Meditation and so-called enlightenment are one. On the other hand, there are the steps.

Note, too, the rather surprising role played by language in the secondary koan, Was ist das Ich? And how the roshi called my attention to the hook in the koan: the neuter gender. ——This shows, too, that the answer to a koan need not be in the koan. It may be there. But in general to say that the answer is there is to say that a "hook," a lead to the answer is there. ——On the other hand, as other things the roshi did will show, it is clear that he could have given this secondary koan and its hook without relying on the fact that genders come out more clearly in German. Perhaps I should say that he could have accomplished a similar result in me without using *this* koan. For I think it is true that this particular koan (as perhaps all koans) depends upon the *Sinn* as well as upon the use (*Bedeutung*) of the koan.[5]

Suppose to the roshi's "Who said this?" I had replied: Paul Wienpahl? I am sure he would have found another way of doing what he wished in the way of guiding me at the time. I am sure of this because of other things he did (such as pointing out that the Zen Buddhist can quote from any scripture to accomplish his *teaching,* his guiding), and from the fact that he gave me the clue to the secondary koan as an afterthought. (Possibly it occurred to him that my German might miss it.)[6]

162, 164: The impression I had at the time of the koan's talking to me cannot be overemphasized. I have tried to think of more suitable ways of expressing the koan's "talking." I have come across several, but none satisfies me the way that phrase does.

163, 164: It was like looking into the koan and seeing the "mu" there for the first time. Before it had always been, as it were, an indistinguishable part of the koan, the recital. Now it stood out—so to speak—as the whole of the koan. ——It was, again, like looking at something objectively, seeing it for what it is.

Seeing the *mu* in the koan = seeing the koan directly (knowledge by acquaintance). (That does it better than "the koan's talking.") In the phrase "know directly" the "know" is closer to that in "Abraham knew Sara and she was with child" than it is to that in "I know that men are mortal." It is the "know" in "know thyself." To think it is conceptual knowledge is to miss the boat. That is why knowing oneself does not involve analysis. Analysis for the self is like dissection for the body: both are legitimate in illness and unnecessary otherwise.

Metaphysics = the science of being.[7] The "science" here is "direct knowledge." Working as though it were conceptual knowledge turns metaphysics into science in the ordinary sense of that term. Hence the oddity of Wittgenstein's practice of philosophy and of Heidegger's remark in "Was Ist Metaphysik": Logic will not do in metaphysics. Logic alone simply will not do in metaphysics.

The problem solved! The trouble is that it has other "forms." The hydra-headed beast.

164, 164: The matter of interpreting is important. Interpreting is inferring, taking off from the given to something else. You want to know what Ecclesiastes says? Read Ecclesiastes. On the other hand, interpretation can help by finally pointing to what a thing says or is. The trouble is that it is so easy to confuse the interpretation with the thing said (or the thing interpreted), as the man in the story mistook the finger (pointing to the moon) for the moon. ——There is here a clue to the relativism-absolutism puzzle.

165, 166: This sort of thing, as well as Hakuin's report, also makes it clear that the process is a lengthy one, possibly interminable. One goes deeper and deeper. Samadhi, too, must be distinguished from satori. (See comment 117, p. 209). Zen teachers stress the importance of the former. I have not experienced it.

In this connection it may be remarked that I am reporting on less than a year's work and only three months of sanzen. Pitifully little has been accomplished and I would not make this report were it not for its philosophic interest. I make no other claims for it. Certainly the definitiveness of some of my remarks must be viewed in this light. I have only gone far enough to know that, as I say, the process is a lengthy one, and has the connections I have indicated with the mind-body problem and the idealist frame of mind. The process is quite matter-of-fact and no one pursuing this sort of study would want to claim that he had accomplished much or was on the way to anything great or exceptional.

The report sounds pretentious and intimate. You cannot, however, get through dualism without letting in the illogical.

166, 166: It had seemed for some time that metaphysics old-style was really an effort to know oneself and not an effort to know reality; that is, that it was not science. With the realization expressed on p. 209 one can see that metaphysics *is* an effort to know reality, for reality and the self are identical. ("Reality" and "self" can be used in the same way for certain purposes. It is a step to do so: the step of seeing through the self, the idea of the self.) In seeing this, dualism is overcome. So metaphysics might also be defined as the overcoming of dualism; in particular, the dualism of language and things, that is, of mind and body.

However, the foregoing is misleading unless it is borne in mind that the "seeing" is not an intellectual matter of a sudden glimpse, but a lengthy process involving the whole individual.

167, 167: Wherever "Zen" is used in English it is useful to ask: Can it be replaced here by "Zen Buddhism" or "Zen Buddhist"? If it cannot, it should be replaceable by "meditation" or "meditative."

The tale referred to on p. 167 contains no news. Here again what is important is seeing these things directly. That is where the practice comes in.

168, 168: One would like this report to end with a climax. It cannot, for there is always something more. The process is not a final one, or rather it has no end except death.

169, 168: The parallel between thinking "nothing" and being nothing. There is the analogy of the physical with the mental: the umbilical cord and the "psychological" cord, sexual love and love. Through the one we see things about the other.

170, 169: If disturbed by the psychological and therapeutic ring of all this, one might ask: What is involved in being empirical in philosophy besides claiming that statements should be empirically verifiable?

171, 170: A calm mind: a mind which does not think when thinking is unnecessary, when there are no problems. Philosophy (in one sense) = thinking when thinking is unnecessary. This helps one to see that the goal is not to stop thinking; it is to stop it when it is not necessary. And it is related to saying that there are no personality or psychological *problems*. There is illness and there is maturing. Philosophical "thinking" may be essential for the latter, but in it one is not solving *problems*. To think so is misleading. And because there is a difference between illness and maturing there is a difference between psychiatry and Zen.[8]

172, 170: If one is inclined to think that concepts are necessary for the construction of what we see, and hence that we cannot see a thing as *it* is, the following may help. We may see some object and, not knowing what it is (not having a concept of it), not see as much of it as we can when we recognize it and therefore can apply a concept to it. However, this simply means that memory is helping us, and finding the word for the thing (recognizing it) helps memory to function. This in turn means that memory helps us to fill in the details of what we are observing from past experience of it. It does not mean that the thing appears as it does because, or partly because, we have formed it with a concept.

I am not trying to refute that position here. All the foregoing does is provide a way of seeing through it. To refute the position I would have to show that reasons for believing it are false.

173, 171: And one might say that the conceptual knowledge of the old-style metaphysician has had, as its use, getting to this direct knowledge.

174, 171: That is, if you want reality in philosophy, which most professional philosophers apparently do not.

175, 172: Many actions can be performed in such a way that they are zazen; namely, when they have in them this element of awareness—awareness that they are zazen.

176, 174: There is another step: seeing that you can become a Buddhist and need not—that it does not matter. Then, if you want to use the Zen method to teach, you become a Buddhist. Then in a sense you also take the raft with you. It is like leaving sanzen and being able to go back to it. To make a lot of fuss about not being a Buddhist is as bad as to make a lot of fuss about being one.

177, 174: Step one: become a man without a position (see my "Philosophical Reflections"[9]). What difference does it make if you have a position? Positions are tools, after all. What counts is whether a truth works.

178, 176: "I have no philosophy" is not quite right. If someone were to ask me what my philosophy is, I might reply: get in touch with reality; and then describe some procedures for so doing and describe how the being in touch "feels" to me. However, no theories.

179, 178: One sees in here the sense in the claim that metaphysical or philosophical questions are often attempts to straighten us out on the use or grammar of a word. Berkeley on the existence of matter provides a good example.

180, 180: This talk of distinctions is a useful way of speaking of Zen Buddhism, calm, enlightenment, and "being in touch with reality." It also relates Zen study to instrumentalism. Distinctions are acts of thought, and a distinction is made for a purpose. Detach yourself from purposes and there are no distinctions. ——The next step is to realize this, to feel it so to speak, as well as see it. That feeling is the feeling of oneness. It comes with being one with reality.

181, 183: Think of the Zen-is-a-liquid metaphor; and painting is painting,.it is simply done differently in different times and countries. It helps with getting over the fear of absolutism, or the absolutist way of talking.

182, 185: One can be bound by the term "goal." One thinks that Zen leads to being goalless and that one should not speak of goals. I have been afraid to speak of goals in connection with Zen, and this has made it difficult to talk about Zen. The point, however, is to use any method that will work, and if you are not bound by "goals" the method used on p. 185 is fine.

183, 185: This shows another manner in which one can get caught up in words. Substitute "life" for "religion" here.

184, 186: Notice how this sort of thing, talk of the Buddha and the eightfold path, can obscure the fact that the goal is quiet, just that and nothing more.

185, 188: It cannot be overemphasized that the goal is calmness. One is inclined to think there is more to it. There is not. There are, of course, all sorts of exotic "philosophies" with high-sounding promises.

It does seem more and more that philosophical problems are pseudo-problems; that is, one can get to the point where one does not work on them. This does not preclude the fact that these problems have a use in getting to this condition. They may have other uses too; for example, getting us straightened out on the use of a term.

186, 188: Other marks that a step has been made: (*a*) it gets clearly expressed (phrased) only later, and (*b*) this phrasing comes to be enormously useful as an expression of the new condition and as a means for bringing it about (examples: "reality feeling" and "in the here and now").

224

187, 189: This factual data also has its uses in the process, for it brings out the fact that there are methods and not *a* method. On another occasion I learned that in the 1930's in one temple the ordinary Japanese kneeling position was used during zazen instead of the lotus position.

188, 191: This use of a text from any religion can be interpreted as thoroughgoing instrumentalism. On the other hand, it may be linked to the roshi's claim that religion is the same everywhere despite the differences in its garments. One sees here the connection between instrumentalism and absolutism. ——The simple fact remains, however: the goal is calm.

189, 191: The advice to penetrate so often given in sanzen may be made clearer as follows. It is as though you keep getting further and further in. And each layer, as in the onion, bears a resemblance to the outer *and* the inner layers. Further, it is a matter of doing it over and over again. (Writing and reading this chapter is a form of zazen.) The onion example helps one to see how, even at the beginning, one might think one was near the end; and how, although there is no mystery in it (the outside of the onion looks like the inside), there is mystery in it (the inside is different from the outside). It also helps one to see how, mainly, the only thing involved is hard work.

190, 192: Notice how well this fits with the dissolution-of-the-self experience, how it might be regarded as an expression of that experience.

191, 192: The adult realizes his identification with everything, with all people. In serving himself he is serving all people and vice versa. As we have noted before, altruism and egoism go by the board. Terms like "political action," "social action," "devote yourself to society," and "devote yourself to yourself" take on another significance. What person is the adult thanking when he bows in all directions?

192, 193: This takes all the mystery out of it too. For this is

225

it: just being quiet. He shows me not by a symbol but by the very thing itself! As he had been all along! The other words were just guideposts.

So the mind-body dualism dissolves. Not dissolved. Dissolving.

NOTES

1. This is done here by rereading the chapters on the koan work together with the following comments, which refer to passages numbered in the margins of those chapters. The numbers as they occur in the present chapter are followed by their page references.

This places a heavy, perhaps unduly heavy burden on the reader. However, the foregoing chapters represent a chronological analysis and I know of no means except this for bringing out much of their significance.

2. By Huang Po. Trans. by John Blofeld (New York: Grove Press, 1958).

3. Carnap's distinction. See Chapter One, on positivism; also Carnap's *The Logical Syntax of Language* (London and New York: Kegan Paul, 1937).

4. Love thy neighbor as thyself. Do unto others as ye would be done by. Of course! These are empirical propositions. One thinks of the time when men did not distinguish moral from empirical propositions. Another form of the dualism seen through.

5. Are we not getting into theory here and away from what I claim I am doing (getting away from theories)? Certainly. But there is nothing wrong with theories and science. As the Zen Buddhist says, you retreat from the world only to come back to it.

6. I should like finally to remark in this connection that the incident of the secondary koan helped to dispel for me the mystique of the koans which one often comes across. Some people are now

claiming that the roshis have not thought up any new koans for three hundred years, and there are moves to publish the answers to the existing koans to force them to create new ones. Surely *Was ist das Ich?* is at least a relatively new koan. In the second place, why not use the old koans as long as they work? Would one urge that we burn the Mona Lisa to spark creativity in today's artists? However, perhaps most important of all, it is not the answer to the koan that counts. The significant thing is its use in meditation, the long, hard work. Knowing the verbal answer to the *mu* koan is no indication that one has "passed" or could pass that koan. Finally, in the move to publish the answers there is a lack of awareness of the creative teaching in the roshis' use of koans.

7. *Webster's New International Dictionary,* 2d ed.

8. I now, in 1970, regard psychiatry otherwise. It *is* different from Zen, but may also be helpful in the process of maturing as well as that of recovering from "illness." Indeed, viewed in one way, mental illness is immaturity.

9. *Chicago Review* (Summer, 1959).

THE QUIET OF WHICH I NOW SPEAK OF IS NOT THE QUIET OF RE-
treat. It is quietness in life. One can stop doing philosophy
when one wants. One can do it when one wants. Therefore, I
can end this part of my work on a positive note.

The main direction of this philosophic essay has been a movement from abstract intellectualism to the particular and to the
real. I commenced by talking about contemporary philosophy
and philosophers. The thinking, though subjective, was at arm's
length: in terms of movements and ideas. Gradually it became
concrete, so that I can now say: *I* used to think this way and
that. Further, at the outset I did not see all that was involved.
It was dualism—in more intellectual terms, the mind-body
problem, facets of which are: the belief that the real is rational,
Platonism, and the problem of the relation of language to fact.
I called the whole the idealist frame of mind. However, the
frame of mind was more extensive than at first appeared, for
there were in it also the ideas of the self and of the ego. Indeed,
the idealist frame of mind turned out to be a frame of ideas,
of my ideas, and to depend for its strength not only on ideas but
also on the emotional attitudes which are parts of ideas.

I do not wish to proclaim the thesis that philosophy is what
we call self-knowledge. I now believe that the advice to know
thyself is vital. However, there are no theses in this book, and
I would like this conclusion to be in the spirit of the book,
which is a report on a philosophic journey toward reality, from
unconsciousness toward consciousness. (*That is* seeing through
idealism.) It is the report of a movement toward knowledge of

the self and of the world, in which it is seen that they can be distinguished, *and* that they can be perceived and felt and lived as one.

It may be remarked parenthetically that each aspect of what I initially called the idealist frame of mind was right in its way. Each was a step toward something further. Consider, for example, the view that "the real is rational (the world is spirit)" (p. 1). It may be seen to be so when you realize that what I took to be real is the realm of discourse. Language is rational, it is the rational. And seeing this was a step on the way to getting free from language and being able to accept the a-rational too. It was a step toward consciousness. Furthermore, as one moves into an existential analysis, one feels the rightness of saying that all is mind and mind is all. These sayings have their uses, as I have found.

Consider, too, "Platonism (there is a realm of becoming and a realm of being or essences)." There is the world and there is language (the self, the subjective). Thinking that there are essences was a step toward becoming aware of language, of the subjective. Words are hard to see, for in use they are transparent. As one becomes aware of them they become opaque and difficult to use, (the self gets in the way when one becomes self-conscious). But awareness of words is part of awareness.

In another of its forms Platonism is the insight that there is a relative world and an absolute one. There are. However, I finally came to see that they are one.

For the rest, and looking at things from the absolute side rather than the relative, there are some scattered remarks I would like to make.

In this book I have not tried to use various philosophical methods in a way that might contribute to egolessness in others, or to make the book itself such a work. If passages often sound that way, it is because I am not egoless and was less so when the enterprise started. This is simply a report on one journey toward egolessness. The various chapters are steps on the way. The work of James, for example, may be used in other ways by other people. This essay is a report on a movement toward (not to) reality, out of thought toward tranquillity. It is made public in the hope that it will point to reality and to tranquillity.

The "methods" in modern philosophy—say Dewey's or Carnap's—are not so much methods as they are variations on a method: the intellectual one. What is needed, even after Wittgenstein, is zazen, or some similar *practice*.

An important difference between Wittgenstein's analysis and zen study is that in the former one strives to get beyond the notion that there *are* mental acts which accompany concepts; whereas in the latter one strives to get beyond all notions— that is, beyond concepts too. The former sort of analysis thus appears as a minor form of overcoming dualism, and the latter a major form.

The mind-body problem has several intellectual solutions, or rather, there are several ways of getting to the intellectual solution which is non-dualism (but not monism); for example, the talk of substance (Spinoza), of pure experience (James), and of looking for the use rather than the meaning (Wittgenstein). However, the body must, so to speak, go along with these solutions or they are empty. Contrary to what I *tended* to think, ideas are not diaphanous. They go down into our very being (guts), as the idea of the self testifies. To overcome dualism, therefore, one must go deep. The matter cannot be held at arm's length. To put it differently, the language of nonduality (note, not monism) must come to be used, not just considered.

On the other hand, contrary to what I often thought in Chapter One, in an existential analysis, one is not trying to get rid of ideas. One is coming to note them and to being able to use them where they are useful.

231

There is such a thing as direct knowing, and it is to be contrasted with interpreting. The latter is a way of pointing to a thing. The meaning of a thing is the thing itself.

Philosophy is to look for the meaning of life. But this quest is overcome; it turns into seeing that the meaning of a life is the life itself. However, philosophy in the first sense is a step to philosophy in the second sense. By the end of Chapter One I thought that philosophic questions were useless and that we should be rid of them. It now seems that we should be rid of them, but they are not useless.

The theme that behavior should be spontaneous and mature runs throughout Chapter One. It is particularly apparent in the sections dealing with Dewey and Wittgenstein. It is related to the Zen notion of living your everyday life. It means to be able to live for the sound of a bell, the sight of a wave, without a sense of importance. The theme, however, tends to make one overlook the fact that we do not, most of us, come to this behavior, being at the same time conscious, without going through philosophy; that is, without first interrupting behavior (life), becoming impractical, and turning within. Simply put, doing philosophy is to become impractical, unempirical, and not behave simply. However, it has an outcome.

Many so-called meaningless questions, the philosophical ones, are meaningless because something in us prevents us from seeing their straightforward answers. It has thus been misleading to say that these questions are meaningless or to think that they are just puzzlements. It has also been a step in the right direction; that is, a step toward being able to see their answers, which are simple. An existential analysis may accompany and succeed the questions; you go on in philosophy after you have seen that you can take it or leave it; but the old questions are still important for the beginner. And the teacher of philosophy must help his students to feel their turning force.

The term metaphysics has many uses. A definition of the word which comes out of my essay is: movement toward direct knowledge.

Logic, epistemology, and metaphysics, as these are taught in the schools, are in one of their uses all part of a larger inquiry: Know thyself. The goal is awareness.

There are no theses in philosophy. One tries instead simply to "listen" and to use any thesis to come in contact with reality. Instrumentalism is itself instrumental.

The outcome of the philosophic essay is complete consciousness. I have not reached the end of the essay.

I should like, finally, to conclude with a note on responsibility. My work is, as I have said, not complete. However, it has exposed for me the grounds of natural morality. I think the kind of strength an existential analysis brings forth results in decency of behavior. This strength comes not only from the particular form of the analysis described in this book. It also wells up from the calm which is found as the depths of one's being are plumbed. Furthermore, although it is obvious that human beings are separate creatures each with his own life to lead, I think that it is also the case—though less obvious in the tumult of workaday life—that each creature and the world are one. There are, if you will, two major ways of experiencing life. In the one we are separate and alone. It is the dualistic way, and it has its function. In the other we are everything. In it our responsibility is seen to be so complete that it is natural. It is natural to revere and to help every thing and being, because it is natural to help oneself.

(Here is another reason why this book can be no more than a report: responsibility cannot be proven any more than the world can be proven. Only propositions are proven. Responsibility must be seen to be believed. And that it exists is a mystery, a fact.)

233

I do not believe that the foregoing remarks on strength and identity imply moral excess. One does not strive always to help oneself, for one is not always in trouble. Usually, unless one is ill, one just lives. Moreover, the strength one can have and the identification with others are matters of degree. And the greater they are, the calmer the individual who has them. They do not lead to excess. On the other hand, they and the responsibility to which they lead are always present; they are constant parts of living.

This may be seen otherwise. I am saying that one does not *do* good to accomplish something, for some purpose (although one may be *taught* how to *be* what one is with promises of reward). One does good because it is natural to do so—because, in Kant's terms, doing good is an end in itself. Living is natural. Seen in this light, it is clear that one would not set out to do good unless one mistook life. To have a moral purpose is a dreadful thing. One is good as circumstances indicate that help is needed. There are problems, but they are practical problems. And one can only wait to see whether their solutions are successful.

As Spinoza had it, there is no good and evil. There is only what men call good and evil.

THE FOLLOWING REMARKS ARE INTENDED TO HELP THE READER. THE explanations given are based on my own experiences with Zen Buddhism in Japan during a stay of only six months plus work with it later in the United States for a year. They cannot, therefore, be taken as generally instructive or authoritative concerning the practices and institutions with which they deal. Furthermore, it should be noted that my interests are philosophic and I am not concerned with writing about Zen Buddhism. Finally, one should keep in mind throughout, and especially at the end, that my experiences with Zen Buddhism are limited—extremely limited when one considers that a full course of zen studies normally lasts fifteen years. The reliability of the conclusions to which I come should be judged in this light. It is not, I think, that they are wrong. There is rather the question of how I would speak after longer experience. However, despite my inexperience, I believe that zen study has definite bearings on issues in contemporary Western philosophy, and that therefore this exploratory effort, with all its inadequacies, may be of interest to others.

In general the pattern of the book after Chapter One is as follows. It commences with a report of an interview, called sanzen, with a Zen Buddhist teacher, the roshi (literally, "old teacher"). This is followed by a meditation report; that is to say, a report of my reactions, during meditation, to what went on during the interview. Thereafter reports on sanzen are followed by meditation reports unless the text indicates otherwise.

A sanzen report always reflects the beginning of a new day. Sanzen, with some exceptions which will be noted, occurred at 5 A.M. and, normally, every day. When it did not, this will appear in the text. Sanzen was always preceded and followed by a short period of formal zazen, or meditation.

Before I explain zazen and sanzen, as the former was taught me and as I experienced the latter, I want to make a further general remark. Because of the nature of the work undertaken, one goes forward, then backward, repeats a step, sometimes ignores what has seemed clear before, often deals in ambiguities, and moves by suggestion rather than by logic from one point to another. At first this shifting and turning and returning will prove vexing. However, after a while a general movement in one direction will become apparent, and I think the shifting and returning will come to have as much interest as any straight-line progress of philosophic argument or insight. It takes a little time to get into the thing, in other words, and the reader should be forewarned that I am not just being difficult, but that this is due to the nature of the thing. Moreover, in the last chapter I ask the reader to reread the whole diary section. That this furthers the study he has to take on my word. This procedure, too, has to do with the nature of the thing undertaken. When it is followed it will be found that obscure passages have been clarified, and that their initial obscurity was not only essential to the work, but that probing it furthers later progress. The numbers in the left-hand margins are used in this connection and thus have no significance until virtually the end of the book. I apologize for having to intrude something which clutters the text, but I found no other way of proceeding in this matter.

Zazen is the heart of Zen Buddhism and of zen study and distinguishes them both from any other practices with which I am acquainted. I think it may be fairly said that one knows

all there is to know in Zen Buddhism when one can successfully perform zazen. Books and other forms of instruction may
be helpful adjuncts when properly used; but with the exception
of sanzen, they are more likely than not to be hindrances to
successful zazen. This is particularly true of philosophical
books.

Zazen is a form of meditation ("zen" means meditation). It
consists mainly in sitting in a certain way and breathing in a
certain manner.[1] The Western word meditation may confuse
one about this, because it suggests a purely intellectual process.
Zazen can be performed anywhere. In a Zen temple compound
it usually takes place in a building especially designed for this
purpose called the zendo, or meditation hall.

Briefly, zazen is done as follows. The description I offer
comes mainly from the instructions of a thirteenth-century
Japanese Zen Buddhist named Dogen. The part about counting
your breaths comes from my own instructor. Select for your
meditation a quiet, dimly lit room. Garb yourself in loose
clothing and obtain several large cushions. Arrange these on
the floor so that you can sit comfortably cross-legged upon them.
Seat yourself cross-legged on the cushions. If you can so cross
your legs that the right foot rests on the left thigh and the left
foot on the right thigh, so much the better. This is the so-called
lotus position. It is, however, a difficult position to assume,
and you may satisfy yourself with getting only one foot on a
thigh (i. e., half into the position) or simply sitting Amerindian
fashion. Use a cushion to raise your rump above the level of
your legs if you wish. It is important to get comfortable. Keep
your back straight and erect; your hands in your lap, the left
hand, palm upward, on the right palm, with the tips of the
thumbs touching. Your head, too, is erect. Keep your eyes open
and fix them on a point on the floor about two feet in front
of you. Raise the whole body slowly and quietly, move it re-

peatedly to the left and to the right, backward and forward, until the proper seat and a straight posture are assured.

Now that you are seated, commence to breathe in the following manner. Breathe through the nose. Inhale as much as you require, letting the air come in by distending the diaphragm. Do not draw it in, rather let it come to you. Then exhale slowly. Exhale completely, getting all the air out of your lungs. As you exhale count slowly *one*. Now inhale again. Then exhale slowly to the count of *two*. And so on up to ten. Then repeat, counting up to ten again.

You will find this counting difficult, as your mind will wander from it. However, keep at it, striving to bring your mind back to the process of counting. As you become able to do this with reasonable success, start playing the following game with your counting. As you count *one* and are slowly exhaling, pretend that that *one* is going down, down, down into your stomach. Then think of its being down there as you inhale and begin to count *two*. Bring the *two* down and place it (in your imagination, one might say) in your stomach along with the *one*. Eventually you will find that you will be able to keep your mind itself, so to speak, down in your stomach. Gradually it will become possible for you to concentrate with more and more success on the numbers. Your mind will wander. You will find yourself carried away on a train of thought, but you will have increasing success in bringing your mind back to the counting. Do not try to keep the "alien" thoughts out. Try instead to concentrate on the counting. If necessary, take note of the thoughts as they come in and then return to the counting. Get rid of the thoughts, so to speak, not by pushing them out of your mind, but by concentrating on the counting. Eventually you will be able to be quiet in both body and mind, and will have discovered how busy your mind ordinarily is. In later zazen, after sanzen or instruction from a roshi has commenced, concentration on a koan will replace concentration on breathing and counting.

The foregoing might be said to describe formal zazen. The beginner normally sits for a half an hour, takes a five minute break to walk about briskly, and then has another go at it. Later the zen student will sit for longer and longer periods without interruption. However, it soon becomes apparent that there is a kind of "sitting" which might be called informal zazen. It can be performed in any position and during many simple activities. It consists mainly in carrying over into these activities the attitudes of quiet, concentration, and awareness and the quiet, concentration and awareness that come to mark formal zazen.[2] Thus, zazen can be performed while seated in a chair, picking weeds, sawing wood, etc. When I refer to zazen one will have to judge from the context, if this appears necessary, whether I am referring to the formal or informal sort. Because there is such a thing as informal zazen, a person can come to have his zen study pervade most of his waking life, and indeed in a sense his sleep. A Zen Buddhist once said: When I eat, I eat; when I sleep, I sleep.

There are, then, one might say, degrees of zazen. This fact has some bearing on the position used in formal zazen. Zazen gets more formal, so to speak, as one approximates the lotus position. In this position the arms and legs are "turned in" and point to the diaphragm, which becomes the center of the student's being. This has the effect of intensifying his concentration and in a way coordinating his whole body with his breathing. The position has, moreover, the merit of great stability when properly assumed. In it one becomes like the triangle depicted here. One has a firm base. The center of gravity is low. It is the center of one's being. There is stability and repose as well as concentration in the position. The figure is not top- or mind-heavy. The position, in fact, symbolizes and in a way is

239

the goal of zazen. One can, of course, practice zazen sitting in a chair with the feet dangling to the floor. However, when you compare the resulting figure with that of the triangle planted firmly on the floor or on a rock in the garden, you get a feeling for the greater concentration, repose, stability, and quiet of the latter.

It is the custom of Zen students to bow to their cushions before commencing zazen and to bow to them every time that they leave them. This can become ritualistic. It can also be a significant part of zazen and all zen study, as will become apparent.

There are five sects of Zen Buddhism. All of them employ zazen. One, the Rinzai sect, and I believe the smallest, adds sanzen to the course of zen studies. The word sanzen is variously used to refer to being given a koan to study, to working on the koan, and to the interviews with the student's roshi in which the student presents the result of his work and is helped in it by the roshi. These interviews are brief and normally occur once or twice daily during times when the student is actively pursuing his zen studies.[3] What a koan is will shortly become clear. Suffice it to say here that it is a question the student is requested to "answer" about some Zen anecdote, or simply a peculiar question, such as: What is the sound of one hand clapping?

There is ritual connected with the sanzen interview which also plays a vital role in sanzen. Of some of this one must be aware in order to follow parts of this book. Before sanzen (the interview) the student is engaged in formal zazen. The roshi is in his quarters in another part of the temple. His readiness to conduct sanzen is announced by the sound of a gong. The students thereupon proceed to line up in a kneeling position outside the roshi's rooms. The first student is then summoned to his presence by a small hand bell which the roshi rings. The student in turn announces his entry to the roshi by sounding a small gong. The interview is terminated by the roshi ringing his little hand bell, the sound of which also summons the next student who, entering, passes his predecessor coming out.

At the door to the room in which the roshi is seated on his cushions in meditation, the student coming for sanzen kneels and bows his head to the floor. He rises, approaches the roshi with his hands palms together before his chest, kneels, and once again bows so that his head touches the floor. Then, kneeling, he recites his koan and presents the result of his work. The roshi says or does whatever is required, and the interview is terminated by his ringing of the hand bell. The student bows, and the roshi returns to meditation. The student rises and walks from the room. This time his hands are cupped before his chest, "holding that which the roshi has just given him." At the door he turns, kneels, bows, and returns to zazen.

There is no conversation before or after sanzen. Indeed, the serious Zen student indulges in no unnecessary conversation at any time when he is actively engaged in his studies, and there are prescribed periods of complete silence. There is also the custom that one discusses one's sanzen with no one, not even the roshi. What goes on in the interviews is regarded as strictly private. There are good reasons for this. One is that the work in which the student is engaged *is* private and personal. Another is that discussion of his koan with another person can, in fact, mislead him and impede the work. A third is that other students may be misled when they come to work on a given koan by what they have heard about it from one who has gone through it, either wholly or in part.

This naturally raises the question of the propriety of discussing sanzen at length and for a public. I feel justified in it for several reasons. The discussion is an integral part of a philosophic essay which was begun long before I knew anything about Zen Buddhism, and which is in some sense broader than the work I did in connection with Zen Buddhism. The discussion of the koan, in other words, is not given for its own sake, but within the context of Western philosophical issues. In the second place, I believe that this entire essay sheds some light on these issues, however little, by pointing to a state of mind. Third, I discuss only one koan, and only a part of that. If what I say misleads others, it can mislead only slightly. And I have enough respect for abilities of roshis whom I have known to believe that any one of them will soon draw a student out of any pitfall into which my remarks may have caused him to tumble. Fourth, I cannot believe on the basis of what I now know that the discussion in this book will finally mislead anyone. In the fifth place, I am not a member of the Rinzai sect and do not feel bound by its customs. But this raises the question whether I am not violating a personal trust with my roshi and with the individuals who introduced me to him, by making these things public. In a way I am not, for I was not explicitly instructed not to do so. However, that is to quibble. For in another way I *am* violating a trust, and I take full responsibilty for doing so. I do it for reasons one and two above. If it should turn out that *Zen Diary* does more harm than good—and we can only wait and see for that—then I have been wrong. I do not believe the book will do more harm than good (probably it will pass unnoticed). Of course I may be wrong, but I do not believe that I am.

At least once a month during each term of active study in a

Zen temple the students (laymen and monks) spend one week in particularly intense pursuit of their studies. This week is called sesshin. During this week temple chores are reduced to a minimum. Every energy is devoted to zazen and sanzen, the interviews with the roshi mounting to five daily. Very serious students may not sleep at all during sesshin, but the routine of the temple at this time is such as to cut sleeping time for the average student to four hours in the summer and one hour during the winter. In a sesshin all communication except that of sanzen is by means of gongs, bells, and clappers. During parts of the day the roshi comes and performs zazen with his students. From time to time he walks around the zendo observing their posture and breathing, their concentration and effort. He makes suggestions and presumably can infer from what he observes a great deal about each student's progress and what is needed to further it.

The only time that I lived in a Zen temple compound was during a summer sesshin. The rest of the time I had private rooms in a temple of another sect and did formal zazen at the zendo of the First Zen Institute in Kyoto. For sanzen I went daily at 5 A.M. to my roshi's temple.

I use the word Zen with an upper-case Z as short for Zen Buddhism or Zen Buddhist, and zen with a lower-case z in such phrases as "zen student" and "zen study." Both Zen students and zen students are engaged in zen study, although the former is a Zen Buddhist and his studies might be called Zen studies. By zen study I mean an existential analysis which includes zazen and sanzen. For other terms such as samadhi and satori, I presume on the reader's acquaintance with them. If he is unacquainted, he will find them eventually defined in the text, or may look them up in *The Three Pillars of Zen,*[4] the only work a student interested in zen study should consult before he is well along with his study.

1. English-speaking zen students often refer to zazen as "sitting." One might say, then, that the heart of zen study is sitting. It may be remarked that the Zen Buddhist also considers the practice of a strict moral code an essential part of his study and his life. However, since in this he is like other Buddhists and adherents of other religions and practices, I take the heart of Zen Buddhism to be the practice of meditation.

2. The activities in which zazen can be practiced are limited by the fact that during it one may descend into such deep concentration that one becomes completely unaware of one's surroundings. Zen students sometimes speak of this as having the mind "drop down." Clearly this would be undesirable while driving a car.

3. As these studies are now carried on in a Rinzai Zen temple, there are two terms of about three months each of active study per year. The rest of the time the student is on his own and may be away from the temple. A serious student may remain and study throughout the year. For some reason which I do not know, a normal introductory course of study is three years. However, the student who completes his sanzen work, in the course of which he may be given several hundred koans, and receives the seal of approval from his roshi, may be actively engaged in his studies for from nine to thirty years. Very few students receive this seal of approval, and fewer still are given the additional acknowledgment by the roshi that they may in turn teach or be a roshi. It takes a man of exceptional fortitude, intellectual and otherwise, to attain that status.

4. New York: Harper & Row, 1966.

70 71 72 73 8 7 6 5 4 3 2 1